PART OF THE SOLUTION / PORTRAIT

OF A REVOLUTIONARY

*You're either part of the solution
or you're part of the problem.*

PART OF THE SOLUTION / PORTRAIT

OF A REVOLUTIONARY

Margaret Randall

A NEW DIRECTIONS BOOK

ACKNOWLEDGMENTS
Some of the poems in this book first appeared in the following magazines, to whose editors grateful acknowledgment is made by the author and Publisher: *American Dialog, Casa de las Americas, Chelsea Review, Consumption, Damascus Road, Direct from Cuba, Doones, El Corno Emplumado, Elizabeth, Evergreen Review, Flagstones, For Now, Hiram Poetry Review, I-Kon, Imago, Inscape, Klact, Kulchur, Liberation News Service, Litmus, Loveletter, Microcosmos, Minnesota Review, Monk's Pond, O.C.L.A.E., Old Mole, Poetry, Rat, Remember Our Fire, Road Apple Review, Solo, Some/Thing, The Village Voice, Win.*

October (1965) and *Water I Slip into at Night* (1967) were published by El Corno Emplumado Publishing House in Mexico City. *So Many Rooms Has a House But One Roof* (1968) was brought out by New Rivers Press, New York City. "The Real American Flag Unfurls with the Help of a Wire Frame" first appeared in *Inside Outer Space* (1970), edited by Robert Vas Dias and published by Doubleday-Anchor Books, Garden City, New York.

Manufactured in the United States of America

First published clothbound (0–8112–0470–7) and as New Directions Paperbook 350 (0–8112–0471–5) in 1973. Published simultaneously in Canada by McClelland & Stewart, Ltd.

New Directions Books are published for James Laughlin
by New Directions Publishing Corporation,
333 Sixth Avenue, New York 10014

this book is for *Gregory*
Sarah
Ximena
Anna
&
Robert

CONTENTS

PART OF THE SOLUTION / PORTRAIT
OF A REVOLUTIONARY

INTRODUCTION / Robert Cohen

—Havana, August 1971
Year of Productivity

It's called "changing your bones."

Something occurred to me today at work: that when you live with somebody, and you struggle, and you love deeply and seize the time and collective place of the relationship, the difference between criticism and self-criticism begins to break down. When you stop feeling so isolated and outside, and when it's no longer "your own skin" to save or hold onto.

How did we get to be the way we are?

•

Margaret has been keeping a diary for over a year and a half, since July '69, when we were forced into hiding in Mexico. The diary contains some of her best writing. And most useful.

This contrasts completely with the diary she kept as a kid, which is really one of the "pure products" of the Amerika Margaret has now dedicated her life to destroying.

Her upper middle-class (lower upper-class) family used to take trips all the time. Margaret's illuminating accounts of these imperial journeys consisted of observations such as:

Lima is extremely dirty.

I thought the train would never make it up the mountain.

I had cramps all morning but ate a big lunch anyway.

Why don't the waiters here wash their hands?

Prices are very, very low off-season in Seville!

Things like that. . .

Makes me think what tremendously powerful forces must be at work in the States (in the world) to allow such a despicable, warped creature to develop into a conscious revolutionary fighter like Margaret!

The combination of events, accidents, decisions, illusions, errors, leaps forward, and suffering going into this process. . .

The famous ripening historical moment. . .how many countless others get caught up in it, "patients" coming out of that heavy class anesthesia.

•

It just occurred to me that her impatience stems from the privileged upbringing she had. Things don't move fast enough for Margaret, because she was brought up thinking you can always get what you want, you need not eat your heart out waiting for something you'll never get. This class conditioning probably is at the bottom of a kind of obsessiveness Margaret has.

(Things don't move fast enough for the most oppressed people either, but for obviously very different reasons.)

There's no question that Margaret had a very privileged upbringing, and that it went right to her bones, but certain variations in the traditional upper-class pattern also had their effect. For one thing, John and Ellie, her parents, didn't consciously identify with the ruling class, or with any particular class for that matter. If anything, they were Bohemians. What probably happened was that they got shaken loose from the crumbly lower crust of the upper class—in the subterranean tremors of class society.

This in-between-the-classes position, this halfway rejection of privilege (liberalism), gave the Randalls a somewhat ambiguous way of life, very contradictory to say the least. So many of Margaret's contradictions must come from this.

Getting back to the point I made before about her impatience being connected to the privileges she had as a kid. Good Puritans (Protestant work ethic), Margaret's parents taught her that you had to *earn* your way in this life. A confusing thing, because her parents "came into money," as they say. By a very Amerikan mechanism, unearned wealth somehow becomes "earned" by means of guilt. But I don't really know how much that applies to John and Ellie.

What I wanted to say is that while Margaret was being taught that nothing is coming to her (taught in words, half-values), things—a comfortable life—were in fact coming to her. While it's true she was early taught the "value of money" (passed on to her as a survival technique, maybe like a worker teaches his son to be *macho*, how to use his fists), there was enough around to buy her just about everything she needed, if not everything she wanted. The ideology and the life didn't go together very well.

2

In Margaret's case (the case of many of her generation and maybe the majority of the next), the terrible contradiction between the ideology and the way of life would be stripped naked. The tremors in the class crust were getting stronger. For a lot of reasons, the contradiction would have to be eliminated later on. The moving-out, moving away, frustrated half rebellion of her parents was picked up afterward by Margaret. She took it South, took it further.

•

Margaret was in the sixth grade when her family moved from Scarsdale, New York, to Albuquerque, New Mexico. She felt lonely and needed to make friends, so she had to adjust to a whole new social pattern, a strange Middle Amerika nowhere culture. She became an Episcopalian at the age of eleven, coming to piety, baptism, and confirmation by way of the Episcopalian Youth Center. Her parents, who sent her to Quaker Sunday School (more for cultural than religious reasons, probably) before, and Christian Science Church (influence of Christian Science practitioner grandfather who collected socks and screw drivers and called beer by another name in order to justify drinking it), were appalled at Margaret's decision to "convert." But Margaret wanted to be popular, and in those days you had to belong to the Episcopalian Youth Center to be anybody, somebody, in Albuquerque, New Mexico. So she "became" an Episcopalian, and also achieved "popularity"—but Margaret never quite made it to being the Most Popular Girl in School. She knew rejection and jealousy. Getting back to religion, Margaret somewhere during this preadolescent period became a "Job's Daughter," a Masonic-type deal which as she herself says was much worse than a religion. It must have been hard for her parents—liberals, with a good deal of worldliness and sophistication, to see their daughter become so tremendously out-of-it, small town, corny: *Job's Daughter*! Margaret, in turn, started hating it that her parents were so different. She wanted more than anything else to fit in. Her parents were "different." So she went through feelings of embarrassment as a result of this. But I remember Margaret once telling me that whenever her father would have his string quartet evenings at home, she'd play Country 'n' Western music real loud to drown out the

3

alien (un-Amerikan) culture of her parents. She loved Country
'n' Western music.

•

Margaret always—always—was afraid of mushrooms. Like Annie,
our youngest kid, seems to be afraid of cats and dogs. No, worse.
Much worse. Margaret hates mushrooms much more than John
Cage loves them. Margaret feels she has to protect herself against
mushrooms. Because she thinks they will get into her. Into her
mouth, especially into her vagina. Into a crevice of her body, under
her chin. Margaret is armored against mushrooms by means of a
tightness and spring-action nerves and reflexes. She can't ever
remember not being afraid of mushrooms. The fear predates just
about everything else. Way before Albuquerque, way before
Scarsdale, way before. . . She traces it back by means of incidents.
Confrontation A, B, C, with mushrooms. And after the incidents
run out, there's the fear of mushrooms.

She's fought with it, tried to conquer it. Imagine what it must
be like to feel uneasy near lawns, frightened in the woods, un-
comfortable in the countryside? A city person.

But neither the commando method (titantic effort to look at,
approach, and reach out to touch a mushroom) nor the psycho-
logical method (mushrooms look like penises—am I afraid of
penises?) seems to have done any good.

Margaret hates to be touched by surprise. When she knows
it's coming, then it's okay. She can then prepare for it (verify
there's no mushroom going to be stuck in her?). It's almost unbelievable, though, what a fantastic difference there is between
Margaret tight and Margaret relaxed and loving. For a person
who closes so completely, her openness in love, physically, her
abandon, is really amazing.

•

In Albuquerque, Margaret was caught in the crossfire of several
apparently peacefully coexistent but really deeply antagonistic
cultures. And classes. Although the cultural thing was much more
apparent.

When Margaret got to New Mexico (1947), Indians were pro-
hibited by law to purchase or consume alcoholic beverages.

4

Alcoholism was, accordingly, at plague level on the "reservations" (which suited Amerika just fine). Gas stations had funky maps telling white tourists where and when the Indians would be putting on their next "show."

During the Civil War, New Mexico sided with the North. There were hardly any blacks in Albuquerque when the Randalls arrived. The small black colony lived down by the railroad tracks, naturally, and the men made their livings as porters, janitors, and redcaps for the Santa Fe line. There wasn't all that much "official" racism in Albuquerque then.

John got to be friends with an Indian. They worked "together" in a clothing store, John out front selling and this Indian out back cutting material, I think. They were friends—within the obvious limits imposed by class and caste. But the thing is that this Indian was no less than the governor of a nearby pueblo, the top civil authority in his tribe. And every morning he'd take the bus into Albuquerque to cut cloth for the oppressor's back. That should give you an idea of the context. It was through him that the Randalls got into their Indian Culture Thing.

Martinez Town, meanwhile, was the *barrio* where the Mexican-Americans, who weren't called Chicanos then, lived. The whites, or should I say Anglos, called them *Pachucos*, which roughly denoted knife-wielding, untrustworthy, inferior, and dirty people.

And there was the Mainstream Albuquerque White Culture, the death culture erected on the ashes of Indian genocide and haunted by the malign spirits of the likes of Henry Ford and Walt Disney. But even here there was a breakdown into strata, classes, which should surprise no one. Margaret tells me there were two high schools in town, one of them roughly proletarian and racially mixed, the other "better."

That's the one Margaret attended.

•

Body politic.

She "developed" late. Like me. I know from my own experience how that is. A "normal" adolescence is hard enough in Babylon. Must be infinitely more difficult for a girl in Babylon, where a woman's secondary sexual characteristics are literally "assets" in the market place.

5

Most of her friends were already "riding the white horse," as they called it, when Margaret first joyously menstruated. She ritualized and formalized the great event by showing her slightly stained panties to her girl friends in the neighborhood. In her junior high school, the style for the girls at the time was to wear sheer nylon blouses with *two sets of straps* showing—slip and bra, the latter naturally being the attention-getter. In Margaret's case her breasts swelled late and never got very big, an "absence" she's felt (been made to feel) to this day. Becoming a woman— the definitions, more or less strict, man made. Made in U.S.A. Margaret was never allowed to feel like a "real woman" (her own way of putting it). The fact that she didn't exactly fit the pattern of mass media superfemininity probably was one of the countless factors which went into her rebellion. A factor. But the rebellion didn't mean a total instant break with the values underlying the sexual pattern. As a woman, Margaret took the well-known "earth-mother" route, with all the familiar and painful emotional rationalizations and concessions that implies. And *never* quite feeling good in her body, feeling shame and inadequacy, jealousy and so on. It was only at the age of thirty-one, stimulated by a new relationship with relative health and real passion, and strengthened by a new collective consciousness developing with the Women's Liberation movement in the States, that Margaret began to penetrate the terrible armor of role oppression.

A *real* woman? Right on!

Look at the tremendous sexuality of her writing in this light. There's hardly a poem that doesn't move in sexual images. In a way, her poems are her body, her "inadequate" body and her alive beautiful body that loves and gives. The tension between the two.

Getting it *out*, signaling (zoology).

A long time before she became politically conscious, she was making political connections. She knew in her bones that Revolution means bringing it all together ("My self is my smallest being; the universe, my largest being"). Our understanding of so many of these personal/political connections is still really primitive. But the Revolution is sold out by any failure to make these connections live.

•

After a year in Spain and the subsequent breakup of her first marriage, Margaret started moving with a group of people in Albuquerque who had a great deal of influence on her. Elaine de Kooning, Robert Mallory, Don and Val Peterson, Robert Creeley—artists and writers, intellectuals. Others whose names don't come to mind now. Elaine and Creeley, and maybe one or two others, had been part of the Black Mountain College community experiment—one of the most serious *if elitist* attempts at creating the basis for a really American culture and a cohesive intellectual community. It was the contact with these people, I think, that deepened and consolidated Margaret's thinking of herself as a writer. Not so much in the writing, though, but in the living.

Margaret went to New York in the fall of 1958. Her intention was to stay there only ten days or so, and then return to Spain. She had a kind of romantic notion that her future was in Spain (first stirrings of expatriatism). She had even bought a ticket for the trip.

But she started looking up some of the people on a list Elaine had given her. One thing led to another—one person led to another —and Margaret was no longer going to Spain. The richness and excitement of the intellectual and artistic scene—the young anti-establishment counter culture, though it hadn't been named yet —captured her.

The three years (1958–61) Margaret spent in New York were very crucial in her development. I think it was there she started to be formed in an all-around way. She lived on the Lower East Side, among Ukrainians, Jews, and Puerto Ricans. Old melting-pot community whose streets naturally weren't lined with gold. While most people like her were populating Greenwich Village (before it became Coney Island), Margaret chose the Lower East Side. Forming part of the first influx of white middle-class dropouts, Beats, Bohemians, artists into the neighborhood. The rent was cheap, and you could get cheap meals. Even though each ethnic group kept pretty much to itself, there wasn't the tremendously suffocating atmosphere of standardized Mass Amerika. There was community, there were roots, there were people who for one reason or another held on to deep traditions, customs, language, as a matter of pride and identity—survival. Radically different from the mass culture of Amerika, a product of Holly-

7

wood and Madison Avenue, a weight on the people's backs. Maybe that's why Margaret—and that first wave of voluntary white poor—chose the Lower East Side of New York to live. Interestingly enough, it was sufficient as *atmosphere*, in the sense that the boundaries set by class, caste, and ethnic background were strictly held to.

Margaret's friends were mostly like herself.

Most of them were painters. Margaret's closest friends were painters, not poets or writers, as a rule. Her attitudes toward *making* were to a large extent assimilated during the period of close working contact with painters like Elaine de Kooning, Pat Pasloff, and Milton Resnick. Margaret always speaks of them as people who admired hard work, dedication, and discipline in art almost more than anything else. The more complex categories such as "talent" or even "genius" were somehow less important. They hated laziness, self-indulgence, and the amount of progress an artist (painter, writer, composer, etc.) would make in his or her day's work would be very important in rating that person. Margaret's relationship with these people was, as I said, a working relationship, even though they used different media to express what they had to say; and even though what they had to say did not necessarily coincide. Working: sharing the work, criticizing it, knowing each other up against the work, with the work up against the cold wall of a society that "didn't understand them," or rather, that had not yet fully come around.

They'd work during the day, combining mostly part-time survival jobs with long hours of *work*: painting, in the case of most of her friends, and writing, in Margaret's. In the first year in New York, Margaret "had nothing to say," or so she often felt. She thought of herself as a writer, a poet, but "had nothing to say." She remembers Milton Resnick telling her just to sit down at the typewriter and sit there for ten hours, if necessary—confident that it would "come." At night, around nine or ten, they'd go to the Cedar Bar, a ritual and institution playing a not-insignificant role in the cultural history of the United States. Margaret ate there almost every night—good cheap meals. A place to meet with artists, people who understood each other. Also a place to look for somebody to love. Or fuck. Despite this community I've been describing, people were lonely. And it was very much a male-supremacist subsociety. Margaret wasn't aware of male chauvinism as a political affliction then, but she was being fucked over by countless artists, writers, intellectuals, plain *men* . . . one night, three days, two weeks, several months . . . it was hurting beneath the fullness of being part of a very creative movement.

I want to talk a little bit about survival. Margaret held down countless jobs in order to support herself while in New York. Here's a rough list:

Sitter in art galleries.

Secretary in Pat Pasloff's father's feather factory in the garment district.

Secretary at American Food and Drug testing company—fired.

Envelope-addresser at the Book Find Club.

Art model.

Writer of reviews for *Art News*.

Court interpreter.

Waitress at a gay club.

The job she held longest and which meant something to her (which wasn't just a way to stay alive) was at Spanish Refugee Aid, a progressive charity organization to help exiles and veterans of the Spanish Civil War, run by Nancy MacDonald, with whom Margaret became very close.

When she first came to New York, she sat in a place called the City Gallery, a tiny loft over a bar started by Red Grooms and several other young artists. They couldn't pay her any money, but she was able to live there. There was no bathroom, so she used the one in the bar downstairs. Nobody ever came to the gallery, so she was able to sit in front of her typewriter for ten hours, if necessary. I think it was that nothing-to-say period. Red Grooms was just a kid then, an unknown painter—now he's famous.

Between jobs, or even during them—unemployment insurance. Beating the system, or feeling as if you're milking it for all it's worth. Like every other American, Margaret felt unemployment pay was "coming to" her.

She would go down to Union Square every morning and pose nude for an old painter who'd serve her a glass of orange juice and who once bought her a pair of galoshes. Although she posed nude, he'd paint her with a little pink ballet skirt on. And when

9

he wanted her to change position, he wouldn't touch her, just point to the part of the body he wanted to move, and where.

Margaret lasted three days addressing envelopes at the Book Find Club and "almost went crazy" from the alienating robotized work. She worked alongside a black sister from the South whom she tried to convince to leave the terrible job that was exploiting her; but the sister said she couldn't leave the job, and in fact said she liked it. Something Margaret couldn't understand at the time. Later, analyzing it, understanding.

As court interpreter, Margaret had her name on a list. When it was her turn, they'd call her, pay her ten bucks an hour (or a fraction thereof), plus taxifare. Good pay. But her name apparently didn't come up often enough for her to live on what she'd earn interpreting. Despite the infrequency, the experience seems to have been very important, in that she was able to be right there where the "legal" whipping and humiliation of Puerto Rican brothers and sisters by the power structure took place. Mostly eviction cases. It was really important for Margaret to see the hatred and rebellion in their eyes.

Margaret worked as a waitress in a club/motel in Amagansett. I was a waiter in a hotel once, so I know how humiliating the job can be, and I remember how much worse the sisters were treated both by the management and the guests. The tipping system is supposed to break you in half, rip out your guts, and leave you a smiling obsequious zombie. Once a customer threw a quarter at Margaret, as a tip. He threw it across a gap only the Revolution will close.

I remember Margaret once telling me that the night she quit that job she decided to hitch back to New York, and she happened to get a ride with an off-duty pig. A pig, it turned out, who liked poetry, or jazz, something like that—a friendly pig. They had a friendly talk and even kept in contact afterward for a while. In Margaret's eyes, in the eyes of White Amerika at the time, he wasn't a *pig*. He was just a nice enough guy doing his job, and the job really didn't seem all that political. Things of course are different now. Cops have always been class traitors, repressive agents, but today there's no illusion about the meaning of that uniform, that riot baton, that service revolver, that spraycan hanging from his belt.

Margaret worked for two years at Spanish Refugee Aid. There

was some secretarial-type work, but her job was mostly case work—old Spanish refugees stranded, broke, sick in France. S.R.A. tried to get them places to live, clothes on their back, medical care, etc. She worked only four days a week, the hours necessary to do the work, flexible. That gave her time to do her writing. Nancy MacDonald ran the show, with a long list of figures and personalities of varying progressive liberal or radical stripes as sponsors. Nancy was good to Margaret, and the job put her in touch with the Spanish Civil War, the glory and tragedy of Spain. With the fighters. The discussions Margaret had with Nancy and Rhoda Waller, a sister who also worked there, were really important in her political development. Of all the work she did for S.R.A. Margaret is proudest of the big art show she organized singlehandedly to benefit the refugees. Through her artist friends, she was able to get big names and not-so-big names, and the show was a big success.

·

The rags-to-riches American melting-pot upward-mobility machine.

By the time she had gone to New York, some of the artists were making it, selling big. Some, in fact, were already rich. Not rich-rich, ruling-class rich. But rich enough. Rich enough not to know just what to do with all that money. Margaret came along just about the time many of them were learning to live with money and recognition, after so many years of relative poverty, shit work, anonymity. They didn't know what to do with that money because it came unaccompanied by power.

Margaret was close with many of the Abstract Expressionists, mostly immigrants or second-generation immigrants.

Willem de Kooning gave a lot of money away, gave Margaret $800 when she was pregnant with Gregory.

She went with him to buy his first suit, expensive uniform for "negotiations" with patrons uptown.

To inaugurate his new studio, de Kooning officially sealed his success by hiring Pinkerton pigs to protect himself against the people.

Franz Kline, who Margaret knew less, bought a car, though he didn't know how to drive. People drove him around.

Power?

The ruling class was in its postwar modernization phase, and was shopping around for a suitable culture to adopt or rather coopt as its own. Madison Avenue's tremendous successes in selling the Amerikan Way of Life gave Wall Street the go-ahead on the creation of a "mass" culture. Not *mass* in the sense of being a genuine culture of the voice of the people, but "mass" in terms of pervasiveness and standardization. A spectacle, a market place, a whorehouse, stage show. There was a continuum established, the two opposite poles of which were symbolized, roughly, by the Museum of Modern Art on the one hand, and Hollywood on the other.

The good, decent, talented, honest, and hard-working artists— the ones who had the integrity to pursue an experiment and a vision in the face of long years of rejection—were fed into the star system that was dazzling Amerika into a stupor of one-dimensional well-being.

It was Allen Ginsberg's *Howl*, which somebody read aloud at a party—back in Albuquerque, in the late '50s—that started Margaret moving with the Beats.

What moved her?

A great HOWL, an eloquent, ugly, human HOWL.

Was that all that could be done in the '50s in the Monster's belly?

If you were white. Intellectual. Alienated. Damaged.

And with new aches and stirrings of history and young life in you.

Maybe the capitalists had educated too many people too well, and now they had a whole generation on their hands they didn't know what to do with, or rather that the system couldn't absorb in the same old ways.

Looking at it from a narrow point of view, many people have characterized the Beat Generation as a "dropout" movement (which it was), without realizing that in a deeper sense the Beats were *pushed out*.

Amerikan society: obsolete, bankrupt, a terrible rich failure.

Beat Generation: a movement to help keep the system running.

Only the capitalists didn't really know where it would all lead to or how to keep it under control.

Just so long as the Beats saw themselves as victims, just so long as they looked inward for richness and escape, just so long as their unity remained a brotherhood of damaged, sacred souls—it was okay, they were given room.

The room was called "life style."

And there was plenty of money to be made there by the entrepreneurs of hip culture.

The Beats were artists in a new sense. Not artists for creating works of art alone, but artists for beginning to create their own lives.

Seeds of Revolution there. . .

The painters Margaret knew in New York were, on the other hand, pretty conventional in the way they lived. Mostly had fairly ordinary family lives and values. Their paintings may indeed have represented a radical departure from the lifeless art that people had stopped relating to long before, but there was nothing radical about the way they chose to live, nor about the values which sometimes determined how they lived. The Beats had started to live out their rejection of the system, and the painters moved with a certain degree of autonomy within it, finding a place.

Margaret overlapped. She thought of herself as a Beatnik but in fact was much closer to the painters.

The values of money security, hard work, monogamy, cleanliness and order, rationality—all of which were rejected to one degree or another by the Beats—were very much a part of Margaret's life and way of being, which situated her with the artists.

But the painters—the Abstract Expressionists—were much older than Margaret.

There was a generational thing at work. Many of her friends were twice as old as she was.

The painters drank a lot; the Beats smoked grass.

Margaret drank and smoked grass.

The painters were more up-front political, in the traditional sense; the Beats were more religious.

Margaret was consciously political. Though she had thrown off religion by the time she was living in New York, she was still pretty mystical, especially in terms of emotions and human relations.

Writing, too, was heavily mystical for her. Dreams, bodies, weather, disembodied touching, depopulated feeling, edges and corners. . .

As a poet, Margaret didn't end up identifying herself with the Beat poets as such, though there was always a relationship, an interchange there. The Black Mountain poets attracted her much more and decisively influenced her way of writing.

Robert Creeley, Paul Blackburn, Charles Olson, among others—and back through Ezra Pound and William Carlos Williams. Something in the way these poets grabbed hold of the chaos and made it work; in the way they looked the hurt straight on, with a cold defiance, writing from their own experience. . .hit Margaret hard, and the voice is still there in her poems. The Beats sang the madness of that generation, jumping in—the Black Mountain poets looked bitterly into the pit, circled round, but said *no* to jumping in.

In a sense, you could say the Black Mountain people stood somewhere in between the Abstract Expressionists and the Beat Generation.

Margaret worked there, and grew from that.

•

Political issues at the time: Ban the Bomb, Free Caryl Chessman, Hands Off Cuba. There seemed to be little concern with the Freedom Rides, Southern-based civil rights struggle getting under way.

Margaret read Marx, Engels, and Lenin with a small group of friends once a week. When the crew of the Portuguese ship *Santa Maria* took over and sailed to Brazil (the fascists hadn't taken power there yet), Margaret and 12 others marched in front of Portuguese fascists' embassy in dead winter. (A pig covering the demonstration lent Margaret his gloves. . . that's where things were still at.)

Cuba was decisive. As the Cuban Revolution defined itself as a socialist revolution, positions were being defined in New York among Margaret's friends. Some, like Nancy MacDonald and her left-liberal-progressive Establishment friends, withdrew support for the Cuban Revolution, seeing their own formulation of Stalinism as a specter haunting our hemisphere. Bourgeois people still halfheartedly pretending to be Trotskyites and anarchists, hating communism like a Kennedy.

When Fidel came to New York, Margaret made a superpaella and took it up to the Hotel Theresa in Harlem, where Fidel had wisely chosen to stay. She couldn't get through the police lines, though, and burned to know that Allen Ginsberg and some of the other stars were in there while she was standing outside with her paella.

When the Bay of Pigs invasion took place, Margaret, Marc Schleifer, Elaine de Kooning, and (I think) LeRoi Jones wrote a short "Declaration of Conscience, by American Artists and Writers" which was signed by over a hundred people and published widely in left newspapers and journals. Apart from a couple of distortions and a few bits of false consciousness, understandable for when it was written, the manifesto rallied support for the Cuban Revolution and made the right political connections. That was ten years ago. Looking over the list of people who signed the manifesto, I recognize most of the names.

A lot of things change in ten years. A couple have become new-type "official liberals," not so very different from the ones the manifesto attacks for lubricating the system with slippery opportunistic Cold War ideology (end of). Some are stars of the Establishment's counter-Establishment. Some won fame and fortune in the cracks of the system without realizing they formed part of the cement holding it together. Staying pure while making it. Staying progressive. Some are now attacking the Revolution from "leftist" positions. But there were revolutionaries and potential revolutionaries among the intellectuals who signed the manifesto. Sisters and brothers who realized that art, politics, and action aren't mutually exclusive categories, who weren't content with just signing declarations of conscience.

At one point, a group of friends, including Margaret, decided to visit Cuba, making arrangements through the still-functioning Fair Play for Cuba Committee. Of that group, only LeRoi Jones had the guts and interest to break the State Department ban and see the Revolution. Marc Schleifer went later and lived in Cuba for two years.

Margaret's political consciousness was mainly a moral awareness at that time. A disgust at the terrible ugliness and brutality of the system, a growing sense of its basic rottenness and bankruptcy.

15

What probably worked against her developing a more political outlook was the illusion that living in a little artists' subculture community was not living in the terribly ugly and brutal system, partaking of the rottenness and bankruptcy. And although that was clearly an illusion, it was an illusion that had a certain basis in reality: it was a privileged community, even though, geographically speaking, it was superimposed over several very unprivileged communities. A kind of spiritual insularity was the result.

Margaret felt tremendously isolated and lonely on this island community, and noticed that just about everybody else did too.

She decided she wanted to have a baby. Not a husband, just a baby. She had been sleeping with this poet she liked, so she decided he'd be the father. He didn't care much for her, and she didn't tell him her intentions until she was well pregnant. He got angry and felt tricked, probably frightened Margaret would demand some kind of support, and he didn't show any further interest in Margaret or Gregory.

Gregory Jason Randall, born 1961. Beautiful strong boy-child!

Margaret left New York in September of that same year. Went to Mexico. She had gotten tired and fed up with the scene, the island—tired of the Cedar Bar culture, the poetry made for other poets' consumption; and also disgusted with all the smug marches for an end to nuclear testing that led nowhere, that made no difference.

She considered herself a Marxist, which was part intellectual rebellion and part romantic stance.

She had already built a reputation, publishing in the "little magazines."

Kennedy was sending "advisers" to Vietnam.

She left New York because she wanted to live differently; she must have wanted to *be* different.

Unwed Margaret and ten-month Gregory went to Mexico.

She thought of herself as a Beatnik, considered herself a Marxist. She was trying to make a go of it. New York had been a dead end. She didn't have any solutions—how could there be solutions when people weren't together? How could there be any solutions with so many of her friends being caught up in the currents—real or imagined or desired—of upward mobility, material privilege?

She immediately got in with a group of poets from Latin America and the States living in Mexico. The group in some way revolved around Philip Lamantia, writer of Beat Generation heroin Catholic poetry. They read poetry to each other in Spanish and English, exchanging traditions and perspectives.

Ray and Bonnie Bremser were in the community, Bonnie working tourists and Zona Rosa locals, strung out, crazy, indifference and sadism toward catatonic infant—poets.

Sergio Mondragon was also in the group. The impression he gave Margaret (or the impression she got) was that he was a very political cat.

He was also a poet.

They got married.

Marriage. As I mentioned before, she had been married way back in Albuquerque, to a crazy guy named Sam. A talented man from a rich family. Sam was a semiprofessional ice hockey player, played all kinds of musical instruments, drove a milk truck for a while, and ended up in a mental institution. Margaret was studying drama at the University of New Mexico when they got married. She had just turned eighteen. He was the first man she'd ever slept with.

She left college after the first year in order to "put Sam through school," and later on Margaret held down several jobs at the same time to finance Sam's shock treatments, etc.

They spent two years in Europe, crossing it on motor scooter, then spending a year in Spain. There she danced flamenco in a cabaret, was a cook in a workers' boardinghouse, learned Spanish well, smuggled diaphragms into Spain from Morocco and fitted them, while Sam got a high-paying job with U.S. Army—a year of this.

Sam used to hit her *while* they made love. If Margaret dared to move an inch or make a sound. For some sick reason, Sam wanted her rigid. Sam wanted her dead!

What a hatred of sex!

Hatred of women! Fear!

And Margaret got to thinking that was how it was supposed to be.

Sam would hit her *while* they made love. With all the wonderful electric appliances they got as wedding presents as witnesses.

I can't picture Sam at all—anonymous, cruel, talented, victimized, dangerous American Sam.

Margaret doesn't like to talk about their marriage. I can see why. I can't really picture Margaret in that situation, so abjectly fucked-over and wasted. Apparently she couldn't either. So after dutifully "putting him through" various medical treatments, Margaret went on her own way.

She heard Sam later became a doctor. . .then lost touch completely.

Getting back to the marriage with Sergio. Margaret brought the horn, the jazz horn of America, to their relationship, while Sergio brought the feather, Quetzalcoatl's plume. "The Plumed Horn"—*El Corno Emplumado*, a magazine they founded and kept alive for years. That had life beyond the relationship.

Sergio was the product of fucked-up family background, loveless and distorted. To a greater or lesser extent, Margaret "put Sergio through" being a poet (then a yogi and finally a pill-taking initiate in some psychiatric sect), much like she had taken care of Sam. Margaret typed very fast and had all the *innate* qualities that make women *natural* secretaries, and so Margaret did the practical things like keeping the magazine from dying, earning most of the living, and seeing to it that things didn't fall apart at the seams.

These same *innate* characteristics were also what made Margaret a "castrating Amerikan robot-bitch" in Sergio's eyes. Sergio also had a tendency to hate women, hence his "philosophy," his perverted Buddhism, which according to him made no provision for female nirvana. His yoga taught him that women are "dirty" while menstruating.

Margaret says the marriage began to fuck up after a year, when Sergio started a long march backward. Backward from politics, backward from responsibility, from sharing, from reality. Finding in several mystical sects insane rationalizations for nonparticipation, nonaction, for woman-hatred.

They had two girls: Sarah Dhyana Mondragon Randall and Ximena Mondragon Randall. Three kids, with Gregory. . .

They lived a life in Mexico centered on the magazine and poetry, marginal politics moving toward consciousness and commitment—expatriate institution, the children, making it, publishing, reputation, North and South of the border, repression, students,

18

maids in the house, a house, car, trips, bitter contradictions, and sweltering illusions. Adding it up.

They had loved each other at the beginning. Margaret loved Sergio, though it is something that's hard to feel because of her hatred and anger today. But even she acknowledges it. People change, needs change.

By the time Ximena was born, the thing had gone sour.

A political distance had been opening between them, but for several years Margaret was

1. unable to see it as political,
2. afraid of being left alone, and
3. convinced that she was somehow to blame for what had happened.

The reason that she couldn't see it in political terms is that she was still unformed politically, in the sense that the political understanding she *did* have wasn't applied to her own "private life," especially life's "mystical" areas—emotions and male-female relationships. Politics was still "out there," Marxism still a tool for analyzing abstractions.

The reason that she was afraid of being left alone was that they had quickly established a life, a family, a magazine, a little bourgeois unit that was oppressive and limiting, but minimally secure and familiar. There was a kind of "vested interest" they had in each other as a "team." Randall-and-Mondragon. Publishers, editors, poets: *El Corno Emplumado*.

Margaret's touch on the Latin American reality through Sergio, at first; his reach into the United States of Amerika through Margaret. For very different reasons.

Also habit, tiredness, dependency, tiredness.

They stayed together longer than they should have. They prolonged the institution mainly "for the kids' sake." Which was a way of institutionalizing unhappiness, anchoring the children in lovelessness and falsehood.

One of the reasons she was somehow convinced she was to blame is that Sergio managed to get her to believe (or half believe) that it was true, she really was a castrating Amerikan IBM-machine man-eating Thing. This included being told every day that she was ugly, fat, and old, and that no man would ever be interested in her again, especially since she now "came with" three kids. The root of her problem, he told her, was that American women don't know how to be *women*: i.e., passive, submissive, sexy, inferior, dumb, and so on.

That went on for four or five years. Margaret struggling to assert herself—hating herself, hating Sergio and the life she was leading.

Her anger, her oppressed-and-exploited-person's anger, her woman's anger: it's cumulative, sedimentary, and she never forgets. Even if she pretends to forget. "In tons, do you hear, I'll rip from you in tons what you have refused me in grams!" (Michaux)

•

El Corno Emplumado was the center. Putting out the magazine was in a real sense the focus of Margaret's life during the years in Mexico. And the magazine was in itself a meeting place for Latin Americans and Americans. Bridge between two cultures. Even the image of a melting pot comes to mind. . . For many years, the idea was to bring together the different currents in poetry, bring together what was "good," no matter what the points of view might be. No matter what contradictions were inherent in publishing poets whose beliefs and actions put them on opposite sides of the struggle. . .the idea being that Poetry was, above all, "above all." That Poetry was all about distilling some human truth so profound, so beautiful, so edifying that the issues of this political life and struggle took their place on a lower, more mundane plane. There was some kind of mystical force uniting the religious ecstasy of a Catholic monk with the tough hatred, loving sacrifice, and triumph of a guerrilla fighter. It was the "end of ideology" ideology in literary form. It was to be the ideology of the New Man, they were saying, and Poetry to be the new voice for the New Man. . .

I don't want to give the impression that "anything went": it was a progressive magazine all along. Early in its history, the magazine published a minianthology of Cuban revolutionary poetry. The poems from Latin America often reflected the revolutionary struggle; more often than not, though, they were the products of intellectuals on the sidelines, as if there *were* sidelines. The poems from the States were a mixture—personal/political—with the emphasis on the personal, the individual vision. There were poems from all over the world in English and Spanish translation. It was a magazine for poets, mostly. I think Mao once said that one of the best ways you can tell if a work of art is any good is by asking whom it is for.

The "melting pot" image isn't really any good, because nothing melted or got together in any significant way. In a sense, the magazine's ideology was peaceful coexistence, dialogue—in a decade of confrontation, polarization, and revolutionary violence.

Under the pressure of events, it began to change. There was a developing contradiction between Margaret and Sergio in relation to the magazine, just as in their married life. It was a political contradiction, and Margaret increasingly recognized it as such. Whereas Sergio's liberal and nonstruggle attitude toward the magazine and his concepts of art were consistent, by and large, with his attitude toward the world in general, Margaret began to reject the static and backward conception of the magazine precisely because it did not coincide with the way she had begun to see things, as the terms of the struggle made themselves clear to her. This led to bitter fights over *whom* to publish in the magazine, though the contradiction was never confronted as to whom the magazine was to be *for*.

A concrete example of the way Margaret's attitude changed, and another of how Sergio held onto the reactionary line, will make all of this clearer. . .

Margaret had published several long poems by a Southern poet. She didn't know him, but she liked his poetry. Then in a letter, the guy showed himself to be a racist. Margaret never published him again. . .

Sergio had been publishing poems by this Latin American poet, when they started to hear rumors that he was a C.I.A. agent and had written articles attacking the guerrilla priest Camilo Torres. They received a visit from two combatants from the same country, members of a revolutionary organization, who confirmed the rumors and urged them never to publish that poet-pig again. Sergio didn't believe it, he needed proof—and he continued publishing the agent.

Margaret fought, but uneasily resigned herself to the phoney solution of publishing two magazines in one—Sergio did the Spanish, Margaret did the English. With occasional overlaps.

This didn't happen in a vacuum, naturally. The Cuban Revolution had won and had survived imperialism's Bay of Pigs fiasco, and was lighting revolutionary fires across Latin America. The

Vietnamese brothers and sisters were demonstrating the limitless strength of a people fighting for a just cause, and the impotence of the world-doomed system of imperialism. Blacks in the United States were moving against the state, forcing the power structure onto the defensive, exposing and sharpening contradictions capitalism was supposed to have "resolved" long before. White youth were massing against the war and the senselessness and poverty of the lives the system had mapped out for them. A new culture with revolutionary potential was being created in the belly of the Monster, with something to fight for, a source of strength and transformation.

Margaret, like many expatriates, was able to perceive all of this *as a whole*, as a single struggle.

She was strategically placed to do so.

The magazine survived for many years, something virtually unheard of for a small, unsponsored literary magazine. Its reputation grew out of this staying-power, out of its uniqueness in crossing two cultures, out of its generally progressive-radical stand, out of its refusal to become a showcase for a single school of poetry. . .

Shortly after *El Corno* was born, the Pan-American Union (O.A.S. culture weapon) made an attempt to gain control of the magazine, just as it had and has done with so many others. They sent a guy named Raphael Squirru to visit Margaret and Sergio. He had a checkbook with him and proposed that the best way his organization could help would be by purchasing 500 subscriptions to the magazine on a regular basis. He said he had loved the first issues and agreed that poetry had to be placed in the service of the struggle to create a New Man. Both Margaret and Sergio told him exactly what they thought of the O.A.S. and warned him that they would never allow the magazine to be purchased or influenced by such an institution. If they wanted to buy subscriptions, okay. . .but that would be as far as it would go. Several issues later, they published a selection of Cuban revolutionary poetry, prefaced by excerpts from Fidel's *Palabras a los intelectuales*, which brought an immediate response from the O.A.S. via Squirru. Obviously, the New Man couldn't be funded if *El Corno* wasn't going to listen to reason. . . Margaret and Sergio stood firm, and the pigs canceled their subscriptions.

In the meantime, Margaret was continuing to build a reputation as a poet, mostly in the States—mostly in the little magazines.

She was also gradually becoming known as a political person, someone who had taken sides, a voice of protest.

That's how I knew of her before I met her.

Anyway, what happened was that *El Corno* began to attract people from all over the world, especially from Latin America and the U.S. Margaret had a chance to meet all kinds of people, but most important is that she began to meet revolutionaries. Some were revolutionaries who were also poets, while others were just revolutionaries. Some had already fought—others were about to fight. Most were Latin Americans. The struggles of these people awoke something in her that the inner, personalized struggles of the Beats, for example, never awoke in her. Something that her own struggles had never moved her to.

Call it hatred of the enemy, love for the fighters. Two sides of the same coin. Her first commitments and risks—were in Spanish. Her political vocabulary is first of all in Spanish. In Latin American. In American.

Parallel to all of this intellectual/political history, naturally, and also part of it, was her daily life. The class struggle is so naked in Mexico, the cover so transparent, the myth of the Mexican Revolution so discredited. The tremendous gap between starving poor and pig-rich so clear and unambiguous, and the role of the United States in keeping things that way just as clear, just as unambiguous. Despite the fact that she lived a privileged existence —maids, comfortable house, car, and so on—there was no way for a person like Margaret not to see it. Delivering babies who had a fifty-fifty chance of living—midwifing in the squatters' colonies—was one of her ways of seeing it.

Margaret had been influenced a lot by the Indian cultures in the Albuquerque days, and in Mexico she continued to learn from contact with nonwhite, non-Western indigenous cultures fighting to survive all over the country. Her frequent trips to the countryside, to the Sierras, to the coasts, were like coming up for air. Long talks about the ancient cultures of Mexico and Latin America with good friend and revolutionary sister, archaeologist Laurette Sejourne, were as much about the present and future, the rediscovery of American Man, as about ruins from the past.

•

All of this led up to Cuba—first visit in 1967, a poets' conference. Here was the turning point. After seeing this wholesome revolutionary society of conscious human beings, after getting a dose of the profound solidarity and internationalism of the Cubans, seeing the changes, the creative power released, the collective dignity of work and struggle—there was no turning back. After visiting Moncada, visiting Minas de Frio (huge school for teachers on the site of Che's command post during the armed struggle), after meeting and getting close to Haydee and Ada Santamaria (sisters who fought in the Cuban Revolution from the start), after being treated like a human being, as a sister and as a poet (poetry's a weapon of the Revolution)—where was there to go but forward?

I don't mean to imply that all people who visit Cuba return home dedicated revolutionaries, that Cuba magically transforms all those who touch her free soil. That would be a very un-Marxist thing to say. No, what I mean is that *Margaret* had her turning point here; she was ripe for the Cuban Revolution.

And she didn't return to Mexico a "finished product," though her life certainly was changed. For one thing, she decided not to take anymore shit from Sergio. She left Cuba determined to put an end to that "living together for the kids' sake" business. After about a month, Sergio moved out of the house, and Margaret began moving out of the fragment and into the whole.

The Revolution was what gave Margaret the strength to insist on the definitive break. This isn't an abstraction. Loving the Revolution, really loving the Revolution above all else, means loving the people, loving the fighters, and becoming a part of that struggle. Loving and serving the Revolution is a process of progressively replacing inside you all the fearful selfishness and defensive isolation of the past with the fighting generosity and collective awareness of the future. After Cuba, Margaret felt part of something. Something big. But the kind of big that doesn't dwarf you.

Margaret reasoned that leaving Sergio, breaking with Sergio, wouldn't mean what he had told her it would mean: aloneness. She faced the possibility of not ever finding a man she'd want to live with again, but it didn't matter in the way it had mattered before. Margaret was determined to make Revolution, and time and circumstances would tell where, when, and how this would

24

be done. The Cuban Revolution taught her it is a fight for life, for survival, those are the terms, and that the enemy's reactionary violence against the people must be answered with every weapon at the people's disposal.

Margaret attended the Cultural Congress of Havana in 1968. The second trip to Free Territory (without Sergio, by the way) confirmed for her that the Cuban Revolution was really as immense, historic, and filled with accomplishment and possibility as it had seemed to her the first time.

After the initial effects of the first trip had worn off, after she had come down, some of the things she was saying about Cuba had begun to sound slightly unreal to her, slightly exaggerated. That's something that happens to most people who plunge into Cuba and then find themselves back in the "real" world of their own countries after only having gotten wet. To know Cuba, you've got to swim. The insidious effect that living in the teratogenic societies often has is to make you feel that the other thing isn't really possible, that Cuba—for example—is only a piece of wishful thinking. . . Besides, the first trip had been, for the most part, a tour for intellectuals, which made Margaret wonder if she hadn't received a partial impression of Cuba.

The second visit, then, not only confirmed what Margaret had been able to see the first time, but was even more of a turn-on. Not only were there new schools and clinics in places she had visited only a year before, but the people were displaying even higher consciousness and collective spirit.

The experience was important for Margaret in many respects. The Cultural Congress was a call for intellectuals to place their work, their talents, *themselves* at the service of the Revolution. While clearly stating that art, literature, scholarship, and research can and must be transformed into weapons in our struggle, it was also clearly stated that "It is the duty of every revolutionary to make the Revolution," a commitment that kicks the pedestal out from under the intellectual and says "*Now, fight!*"

The Congress concentrated on problems of the Third World, and the overwhelming majority of sisters and brothers invited to participate were from Third World countries. It was an intense experience for Margaret, another saturation in the fighting Third World context.

She spent most of her time with a group of Argentines, including Celia Guevara, Che's sister, and Pepe Aguilar, one of Che's childhood and lifelong friends. Che had been killed in October, and now it was January. The Heroic Guerrilla's presence could be felt in Havana. Among the Argentines, naturally, the presence of Che was strongest, but the questions raised by the Bolivian experience were being discussed by *all* the delegates to the Congress. What was the meaning of Che's death? What lessons could be drawn? Was there anything basically wrong with the strategy Che had put into practice? What should be the response of revolutionaries to Che's betrayal by the Bolivian Communist party? How could Che's murder best be avenged?

The atmosphere was electric, as Margaret often says.

One important thing Margaret had to confront in Havana was the fact that *El Corno* was considered a magazine for dilettantes, basically, by Latin American revolutionary intellectuals. They saw, of course, that it was a progressive magazine. But they told Margaret that the magazine had systematically been publishing the nonstruggle hippies, the mystics, the elitist poets in each country, only rarely publishing the poets really involved in the struggle. Revolutionary criticism from brothers and sisters. Margaret understood how backward the magazine was.

These opinions came, for the most part, from people who only read half of the magazine—the Spanish section, which Sergio edited almost exclusively. Those who read both Spanish and English apparently saw that Margaret's consciousness—as reflected in the English half of the magazine—had been developing more fully, in the right direction.

This opened Margaret's eyes as to the absurdity of the situation concerning the magazine—which had become two magazines, with two increasingly different points of view, under one cover. She understood how liberal it had been to accept such a situation, how individualistic to have thought it was all right just so long as *her* part had the correct point of view. It's not enough to "be correct," as if the Revolution simply consisted of adopting, individually, a *position*. A position that isn't moving through struggle is just a *stance*. So she resolved to really struggle with Sergio over his editorial and political confusions.

Getting back to the Cultural Congress. Margaret was present at a meeting of Americans and Vietnamese, a meeting she found exceedingly frustrating because of the lack of unity among the Americans and the irresponsible behavior of many of them. A day or so after, she bumped into the Vietnamese brother who had spoken for the Vietnamese delegation. Huy Can, Vice-Minister of Culture of the Democratic Republic of Vietnam. She told him, through the interpreter, how difficult the previous meeting had been for her and how painful it was for an American to meet Vietnamese brothers and sisters, knowing the American people weren't fighting hard enough to end the war being fought in their name. Huy Can said he understood what she was saying perfectly—and without further words threw his arms around her, gave her a ring made from the metal of downed American planes. . . beautifully expressing solidarity with the American people and optimism about the outcome of our common struggle.

The Cultural Congress of Havana issued a final declaration which defined the intellectual's responsibility toward the Third World and set forth a kind of blockade-in-reverse policy, a cultural isolation policy toward imperialism. The delegates pledged not to accept grants, awards, or employment from imperialism, in all its agencies and masks.

That took Margaret a long way from the days in New York, where upwardly mobile intellectuals had thrown in their lot—wittingly or unwittingly—with the oppressor. After the Congress was over, she spent a week with a Cuban photographer in a Havana neighborhood, talking with people of the community. Storing up strength for the return home.

•

Margaret returned from Cuba in January, and I arrived in Mexico in February '68, armed with a list of addresses of friends of friends and contacts for what was going to be a Latin American journey (I was looking for my Sierra Maestra). I never got farther than Mexico. Margaret's name was on the list.

Everybody in New York had told me to look up Margaret Randall. There was a romantic expatriate literary/political aura around that name for me: she was, like *El Corno*, something of an institution.

Once you get to know a person as well as I now know Margaret, it's extremely hard to remember what it was like *not* to know her.

What it was like to see the face I now know so completely for the first time. . .

We met toward the beginning of March. She was obviously still under the effects of Free Territory, radiant, and filled with enthusiasm for some political work she was doing at the time. I guess I couldn't have caught her at a better moment. As for me, I had been expelled from the entrails of the Monster; Amerika had gotten rid of me as easily as a fart. I had felt I was being eaten up alive in New York—the poetry scene and the antiwar movement I was involved in were equally alienating and suffocating to me. I had fled revolution looking for Revolution. In Latin America. As for my political development, I hardly understood anything, except that Amerika was a hellhole, and that imperialism and racism were evil. I had earlier flirted with the Establishment cultural world—perhaps whored would be the better word. I renounced that as fully as I could. My personal relationships were either superficial or tormented. That's a little capsule summary. . .
I go into all of this to give you an idea of what it was like for such a person to meet Margaret, who seemed (alongside me) to be Clarity and Purpose personified, whose life appeared to be the very opposite of my own.

We became friends.

Margaret turned me on to Revolution, to the Cuban Revolution, to the Latin American Revolution. We talked a long time about Cuba and Latin America, about Che, about armed struggle. She told me about Otto Rene Castillo and Javier Heraud, Latin American guerrilla-poets killed fighting for their peoples. We talked about the States, the Chicanos, the Black Liberation struggle. It was a complete turn-on.

It was in Margaret's house one afternoon, together with two Latin Americans, where I agonizingly dropped my burden of "pacifism and love" that had been part of the hippie hype. I was made to realize what the concept "enemy" really means, in terms of flesh and blood and history. Margaret shared that awakening with me and encouraged me in using that new knowledge.

We became lovers. Decided we'd stay together for a while.

Things happened fast. We became a family. With three kids! Outasite!

It seemed real easy at first.

I got a job and kept it, learning Spanish. It meant a lot for Margaret that she didn't have to "support" the family. She could hardly believe she "had" me, secretly fearing this young guy would get sick and tired of all the responsibility and weight of a family, and run off somewhere.

Sergio left the magazine. Margaret and I did the last couple of issues of *El Corno* together, changing the nature of the magazine, trying to make it a revolutionary weapon.

Our activities centered on the house, the kids, the magazine, several friendships, job, several trips, discovering each other. A generally bourgeois life with hatching revolutionary ideas.

We rejected mysticism but were in fact mystical in our love. We lived out the tail end of our Beatnik and hippie phases, respectively, while rejecting the premises of both ways of life as escapist, parasitical, and so on. We balanced on the line between "personal liberation" (self-discovery and disguised hedonism) and revolutionary commitment.

Our life together in Mexico, compared to what it has been in Cuba, was relatively slow paced and simple, which is not how it felt while we were living it. It is indicative of the fact that we develop in stages—I mean we felt our lives were full, when in fact—in retrospect—we weren't drawing on a quarter of our energies at the time.

It seems to me to be very significant that at the beginning Margaret provided leadership in our relationship, leadership based on experience and consciousness. I felt respect and even awe for her. Margaret was nine years older than I, she had three kids, had been to Cuba, was friends and had worked with revolutionaries and guerrillas from Latin America, was a good and prolific writer, had delivered dozens of babies in dirt-floor shacks with chickens getting in her way; her ways were strange, the way she talked. . . she moved in a different world. All of these things made me look to Margaret for orientation, for *context*—since I had rejected my own, was moving out of a context I hated and had been unable to fight to change. Margaret's *practice* offered me a world, a Revolution I had slowly, clumsily been looking for.

This leadership thing was at the very beginning, before we became lovers. And it wasn't leadership in action, unfortunately; it was more of an understanding between us, a recognition. This broke down, began to break down after several months of being together.

As I said before, Margaret had been fully prepared never to live with another man after breaking up with Sergio. She didn't *want* to live with another man if it was going to mean being cut up in little pieces again. But it hurt, it was lonely to be alone. You're not whole if you're not loving, either. So when I appeared on the scene, when we fell in love and decided to live and make revolution together, Margaret felt a combination of gratitude and unbelief: gratitude to me for doing what seemed to her to be the impossible (loving her, wanting to do it together), and unbelief that it could be real and lasting. This distortion placed a limit on the amount of leadership she would be able to exercise in the relationship, while I was working to undermine her leadership in every way I could.

As soon as the monogamous thing got settled, the roles began to settle into the "normal" pattern of male supremacy/female passivity. Margaret's strengths became threats to me and served only to highlight my weaknesses; I used my strengths, in turn, to intimidate Margaret and make her feel stupid and worthless. Instead of complementing each other, giving each other strength and helping each other overcome our weaknesses—we began waging a cold war which set very definite limits on the relationship.

But that's upside down—it was the kind of relationship we had, the institutional limitations of the bourgeois structure, that made for such destructive role struggle.

Cold war—with tremendous love, daily sharing and growth, learning, learning. Fights and breakthroughs. Margaret fighting against male chauvinism in me, destroying the passivity and defensiveness and sense of inadequacy in herself. A really hard struggle, with slow results, backsliding, tiny advances. Margaret always a step ahead of me, natural in a person who's been taught her whole life to anticipate the next blow.

The experience radicalized us, rounded us out, armed us for more struggle. At the beginning, Margaret was Practice and I was Theory (what phoney, impoverished roles!). We battled against that artificial distance, fighting the past's battles. It has taken a lot of changes, objective transformations, accidents, birth, and repression to help us out of that blind alley.

When we first got together, Margaret would joke a lot about how she had never felt like a "real woman." It was an embarassed joke because it meant half admitting that the prepackaged model of Woman being sold by Amerika—the Frozen TV Woman—had done its terrible work. I didn't really understand it at the time, but in retrospect it seems to me that her insistence on telling me, her ritual repetition of the "I-never-felt-like-a-real-woman" half joke, was a way of telling me how much she hoped I wasn't going to hold her up forever against that impoverished yet seductive model of womanhood that every other man in her life had secretly or otherwise cherished and used to crush her with. Fear of ugliness and age, fatness and chin hairs, potbelly: dealing with that.

Counteracting that was the normal, healthy loving that enabled us to see what another human being is actually like, and to understand that desire means moving to meet another person's needs along with your own. Passionate and friendly love, sexual oasis, source of energy and relaxation again and again. . .

Later on, that abyss of inadequacy Margaret was always confronted with in herself, and pushed in by me at my worst, became collectivized as she saw, through the young Women's Liberation movement in the States, that it wasn't an individual problem at all.

Margaret drew strength from the Women's Liberation movement from a distance. And the distance between Mexico and the United States in terms of sexism and *machismo* would have to be measured in light-years. Margaret absorbed the material on Women's Liberation that sisters were sending us. Reading. But after closing the books, finishing the pamphlets and articles and manifestos, there were no sisters conscious of the problem (or rather, the solution) around to join in struggle. The sisters who were nearby —some of them revolutionaries—were moving in another context entirely, or were in some way tied to fucked-up relationships, or rejected Women's Liberation entirely as splitting the revolutionary movement. . . So Margaret had to struggle alone.

So many contradictions. . . I remember how in Mexico I'd make fun of her for being supermonogamous (saying she was an uptight bourgeois wife), as I enjoyed my man's sexual privilege-freedom to be with other women. I taunted her with "liberation," shot off at the mouth about the need to smash the family, while indirectly enforcing the bourgeois code by means of an invisible system of countless little rewards and punishments. All of this

31

left her feeling more inadequate, confused and outraged. Enraged. It took a year or so of many changes to get through to the other side—for her to righteously challenge the monster privilege of double standard in me. I was struck impotent for two whole months when she finally did.

•

The Student Movement in Mexico began innocently enough on July 26, 1968, with a street fight between rival high school groups. The cryptofascist Mexican State seized on the opportunity to "stabilize" the country for the Olympics, scheduled for mid-October. Mexico was "stabilized" with a blood bath the magnitude of which still seems not to have sunk into the consciousness of people all over the world. The killing of August and September reached its climax on October 2, 1968: the Tlatelolco Massacre, in which over 400 people (not just students) were slaughtered when the U.S.-trained Olympia Brigade of the Mexican Army methodically surrounded and attacked a peaceful rally in Mexico City.

"You ask why the poems
do not speak of the soil
of the leaves,
of the great volcanoes of my own country

"Come. See the blood along the streets.
Come see
the blood along the streets.
Come see the blood
along the streets."

I left Mexico in mid-August and returned toward the end of September, so I missed the most crucial period of struggle, during which a mass movement was born and was fighting to stay alive under very difficult conditions. Margaret was very active. In addition to support activities (money-raising, obtaining supplies, etc.), she participated in one of the thousands of street brigades which were essential in getting the news out to the people (through the total media blackout) and in explaining the demands and goals

32

of the Movement. It was a very courageous thing for Margaret to do as a foreigner in Mexico, especially when the pigs were frantically pushing the "outside agitation" line in order to discredit and undercut the Movement, desperately looking for *extranjeros* (or even Mexicans with foreign-sounding last names) to pin the blame on.

We published an editorial in *El Corno* protesting the terrible repression, which led the government to cut off the monthly subsidy the magazine had been receiving over the years (the Mexican government has cleverly "supported" publications as a means of eventually doing away with them), a loss we welcomed and which we made up for through help from friends everywhere. The magazine lived several issues more, publishing things which won us the hatred of both the Mexican and Amerikan pigs.

The morning after Tlatelolco, at dawn, we went to see some of the students we had been working with, at the house where they were hiding. They had all been at the rally. We sat with three of them in the most bone-cold silence imaginable, waiting news of the other comrades, waiting to find out if they were dead or alive. Shortly after, one of them arrived, pale as a ghost and shaking all over, telling how he had played dead for hours in a pile of dead bodies and later escaped into one of the buildings adjoining the plaza where the massacre took place. He brought news of the other brothers and sisters, all of whom had gotten away safely. He told us how he saw children cut down by machine-gun fire, a pregnant woman bayoneted—total fascist mayhem.

This was a really crucial experience for both Margaret and me, as you can imagine. Our righteous hatred of the enemy blossomed, our love for our comrades and the fighting people grew a thousandfold.

Another really crucial experience was finding out that a very close friend of ours, someone Margaret had known for years in Mexico, is a pig. Definitely a pig. And definitely a close friend. This is something that's extremely hard to understand if it hasn't happened to you. And this is something every revolutionary movement has got to relate to in a serious way. Without allowing ourselves and our relationships and our organizations to turn to stone, we've got to find ways to recognize, isolate and punish pig infiltrators and informers. Much better yet would be to prevent infiltration altogether.

This pig was a close friend, maybe not as close as some of the friendships we've developed since, but close enough. This pig had won Margaret's love and trust years before, and I kind of inherited the friendship from her (as a function of my love and trust for Margaret), kind of skipping the necessary process of getting to know somebody. This pig's genius was her ability to make us feel that she felt the same things we felt, that the same things excited, angered, sorrowed her as moved us. She was warm, effusive, confidential, extremely emotional, and most of all—passionate about the Revolution. The fucking pig! And she had "served time in jail," had been "tortured". . . she had a *perfect* story and her life seemed impeccable. . .

All things considered, it was a good thing to have happened. Having no illusions about the enemy includes knowledge of the great lengths to which the enemy will go, the great depths to which the enemy will stoop in the pursuit of pig objectives. There are people who seem to think the enemy is an abstraction, a mental construct without flesh and bone. It was extremely instructive for both of us to uncover a pig in our own lives. Knowing more of what the enemy is capable of arms us with that much more power to destroy the enemy. The experience also caused us to think a lot about all our relationships, about the concrete things which cause us to relate to some people but not to others, about trust and love and what ways there are for telling whether or not people are what they seem to be. . .

I remember when it was decided for security reasons not to break off the relationship immediately, Margaret became sort of obsessed with wondering what it was going to be like to see the pig again. What it would feel like. I remember Margaret telling me, after we saw her, how easy it had been, how surprisingly easy—even to kiss her. There was no feeling left, only hatred. A cold and calculating hatred. She said she felt as if imperialism had ripped out her heart. The experience helped take away some of the romanticism that distorted our vision of what Revolution is all about.

•

Margaret got pregnant in the summer of '68, carrying growing life inside her through the bloody fall months of the Movement, and finally giving birth on March 13, 1969. The pregnancy brought us closer, especially toward the end when the baby started kicking and rolling around, and Margaret had to stay in bed for the last two months for health reasons. Now this may sound somewhat exaggerated or romantic to you, but I saw Margaret's strength when she was on the delivery table when Anna was born. I have seen her strength many times, I've seen it almost daily in one form or another, but rarely have I seen such an example of toughness and joy as during that wonderful delivery (which I witnessed and participated in as much as I could). . .

Now we had four children, four teachers.

•

To know what something tastes like, you have to taste it. It's that way with repression too.

This will be written in shorthand—otherwise it would require a book in itself. . . In the spring of '69, Margaret and I decided we would go live and work in Cuba for a year or so. The situation in Mexico had become exceedingly difficult: a kind of numbness descended on the people after Tlatclolco. The small amount of help we were giving a group of students seemed (and was) terribly inadequate, but nothing else opened up. We made plans to continue editing the magazine from Cuba, with a friend in charge of production and distribution back in Mexico. Margaret received an invitation, and we decided to accept. Cuba—we were ecstatic at the prospect.

The repression hit in July. It started with the robbery of Margaret's Mexican passport by a clever agent who gained entry to our house with false credentials. (A Mexican passport. . .she had changed her citizenship during her marriage with Sergio. . . an unwise thing to have done, it turned out. . .) We figured the pigs would go to the trouble of robbing her passport only if they felt they could hurt her in some way having it in their possession. We realized, for example, that it could be "found" at the scene of some pig-produced bombing. At any rate, it was an effective way of keeping us from going to Cuba, keeping us handy. From a number of things that happened, we became convinced Sunny

Mexico was acting on orders from the Amerikan embassy throughout the whole business. . .

Margaret immediately applied for a new passport, absolutely sure it would be denied (why would the pigs bother stealing her passport if they were going to issue her another one?). At the same time, we reached official circles through various routes to find out exactly what the pigs were trying to accomplish and to put pressure on them to issue a new passport. Dead end. The foreign minister pig himself even told a group of writers that petitioned on Margaret's behalf that the case was too difficult for him to handle. . .

Things got hot, and we were advised to go into hiding right away. The house was being watched, we were followed, there were phone calls. With four kids, you are very vulnerable to pigs who would just as soon kidnap and torture your children as drink a glass of water. Friends helped us out. But hiding with four kids (one of them a tiny infant) is very difficult, if not impossible under most circumstances—and at any rate, it was dangerous, making it harder for us to move. It didn't look like there was going to be any immediate solution. The legal and semilegal channels were slow going. People advised us to be patient. We got word that the pigs had threatened the people taking care of the house. The fact that I was above and below ground, taking care of the contacts, made it dangerous for the kids—I could've been followed back to the house where they were staying with Margaret. So we made the extremely difficult decision to send the kids—all four of them—to Cuba without us. For their safety and our mobility. Anna was three months old. Ximena was five, Sarah six, and Goyo eight. It was a hard decision to come to, but there was no question that it was the right one. . .

The Cubans were fantastic. They accepted the kids without question. On July 25th, the children were sent to Free Territory in the care of revolutionaries. They were sent to a vacation camp where the kids of some foreign guerrillas were staying. . . very well loved and taken care of.

A lesson in internationalism Margaret and I won't ever forget. . .

We were in hiding for almost two and half months. We went through all kinds of changes during this period.

The legal and extralegal pressures being brought to bear on

the Mexican government to stop the harassment and issue Margaret a new passport came to nothing.

Margaret was fairly consistent in rejecting the idea that the problem was going to be resolved through legal channels. Her analysis of the situation, plus a strong, sure political intuition about the way the enemy was moving, told her not to entertain any illusions about Justice being done in Mexico. The Tlatelolco butchers weren't going to worry about the unconstitutionality of denying a citizen the right to a passport.

If she consented to go through certain legal and semilegal motions, it was only because we were urged to do so by trusted friends, and because no other course was open to us immediately.

One idea was to threaten the government with an international scandal over the case. Writers, artists, and intellectuals from all over the world would come to Margaret's defense. But she recognized that a government capable of slaughtering 100 odd unarmed citizens in the presence of dozens of journalists from everywhere (who were in Mexico to cover the Olympics)—some of whom were wounded in the attack, and others who were jailed and beaten later—that government couldn't give a fuck about scandals or protests.

But because of the ambiguity of the form of repression they used against Margaret, the strangeness of the way they chose to get at her, there were periods in which these truths became obscured.

We experienced rage, frustration, fear, and confusion in rapid succession, and frequently all at once. Instead of really supporting each other, we used our doubts and anxieties to score points on each other. Instead of counteracting each others' maddening fantasizing, we took turns encouraging sterile speculation and paranoia in one another. We took our tensions out on each other.

But the experience brought us closer together in many ways, despite these problems. We stuck it out together, found a way out together.

I remember we made love like we never had before, like animals, humans—in the face of a possible separation, or worse.

Discovered in each other an unshakable commitment, to the Revolution and to one another.

There were lessons learned, really learned, unforgettable.

Lessons about friends and lessons about enemies.
Also important lessons about the in-betweens. . .

Some people help you out in a situation like that by opening
up their houses, important help; and there are some people who
open themselves up, giving the kind of human help/political help
that makes you stronger and less liable to make costly mistakes.
We realize the importance of not being alone when the shit
falls. . .

We stayed in several places, including a hotel. Margaret had
been in bed the day the pig offed the passport—sick with what
we later found out was a dying kidney that finally got removed
in Havana. . .and she was sick and in pain on and off during
the two and a half months in hiding. She was alone a lot of the
time, since I was taking care of the contacts who were trying to
solve the problem. She learned something about patience during
the long hours I'd be gone—she not knowing what was happening to me. It would have blown my mind to have been in her
position, but she related to time, not knowing, boredom, and isolation with a perspective and maturity I had never seen before in
anybody, so close up.

Margaret didn't know what was going to happen. Since in
Mexico anything can happen, we didn't discard any of the possibilities. It was possible that the Mexican government had accom-
plished exactly what the C.I.A. wanted: fuck up our lives, stop
publication of the magazine, etc. But it seemed more likely that
what had happened was Stage One of a plan that could easily
have included jail or even death. If you think this is exaggeration
or melodrama, visit Mexico. Talk to people there.

Many people would have doubled over, inward, with fear. Fear
breaks some people up. Margaret dealt with her fear in one piece,
which as far as I am concerned is the definition of *courage*. She
went to work.

She began a diary of all the inward and outward events that
were happening. It ran to over 200 pages. She wrote an autobiography sixty pages long in about forty-eight hours of almost
nonstop writing, answering the pigs with a life. Margaret was on
fire, getting it all down in case something happened to her.

Vibrating, as the Brazilians say. She compiled an anthology of documents from the U.S. Women's Liberation movement, writing a long introduction. *Las mujeres* was eventually published in Mexico, bringing important news to Latin American sisters (and brothers). . . Margaret and I translated Jorge Ricardo Masetti's book about the Cuban Revolutionary War called *Los que luchan y los que lloran* ("Those Who Fight and Those Who Weep"), and poems by Latin American revolutionary poets. . .

Heavy time, passing. . .

We missed the kids terribly, longed for them. We worried about them, each in a special way. We hurt for little Anna, though we knew that at three months her changes would be less painful. News of them was sporadic, but we got word they were being taken care of and being loved. Several of Margaret's friends in Cuba really came through on that score. A couple of letters from one sister, especially, filled us with shame for having doubted that the kids were really being given good care, and filled us with new and deeper love for the Cuban Revolution and the people making it. . .

The two and a half months passed very slowly. Toward the beginning of the second month, it became clear the Mexican government "couldn't do anything about the case," and we made arrangements to get Margaret out of Mexico without the fucking humiliating passport. Margaret took her "constitutional right to travel" into her own hands.

•

After a roundabout journey, we arrived in Cuba, separately, in October '69, and were reunited with the children.

Cuba! For Margaret, it was like coming home.

It was a joyful reunion.

You can get a good idea of her response to this by reading the first two poems included in this volume ("Everyone Comes to a Lighted House" and "New Eyes"), which are about breaking open anew to absorb the new order of things. Overthrowing the fears, subterfuges, conservatism, and bourgeois tastes of the past in order to become part of this revolutionary people.

Joyful—getting the feeling of it again, riding the bus, talking to people, friends—but this time from the inside, living it. Very

39

different from paying a visit, attending a congress of intellectuals.

During the first few weeks, we could hardly believe the things we saw around us: a country really turned over to its people!

It is a mind-blowing thing to live in hiding for over two months and then be living all of a sudden in a society that supports you, that you are a part of, that enriches and strengthens you.

Some adjustment was necessary.

Cubans had had eleven years to grow with the Revolution they were making; we landed in the middle of it, creatures from another planet.

The repression didn't end when we got out of Mexico. We took it with us, especially me. I took it out on Margaret and the kids. On top of that, my uptight *macho* response to this new and demanding reality was to try and be superrevolutionary, which expressed itself as "leftist" extremism, dogmatism, and the worst kind of intolerance. This is understandable, I suppose, coming out of a fear of being incompetent, of not being able to live up to the Revolution. This made for a very bad situation between Margaret and me, and between myself and the children. It clouded what should have been a clear day. Margaret's response to Cuba was much more natural and mature. More human, more revolutionary.

Take her response to the kids, for example. She consistently understood the unbelievable changes they had been put through, she related to their needs and helped them wherever possible to move with the changes. They had spent what to them must have seemed an eternity without their parents, not knowing if we were dead or alive, in jail or on our way to rejoin them. They had grown up feeling special, in a family and progressive school environment that placed a great deal of emphasis on individuality and free expression—in Cuba they found an environment stressing the collective and requiring discipline. They had been taught to hate the pigs, the Mexican government and the *Yanquis*—in Cuba they had to relate to patriotism, respect for authority and internationalism. Even the cultural thing must have been difficult —Gregory's shoulder-length hair, which in Mexico had one political/cultural meaning, meant something else in Cuba. There was no place for it in the highly disciplined school the kids attended. The thing is that the kids took it all in stride, with only minor agonies and momentary traumas. But in my weird defensive zealousness, I would vamp on the kids whenever they'd complain or hesitate. And I would attack Margaret for showing the slightest support for them, for recognizing their needs. I would accuse her of being liberal, of giving in, of making concessions—everything became a matter of principle. Or what seemed to me to be principles.

This fucked-up initial response to Cuba on my part led me to be entirely uncritical of the Cuban Revolution.

Margaret, on the other hand, was able to distinguish between positive and negative. And she increasingly related to people in a natural, spontaneous way.

We both got jobs shortly after arriving. Margaret started to work for the Book Institute, where she's still working. After almost five months of living in a hotel, we were given an apartment. We chose to reject the special rations foreigners are entitled to, preferring to integrate ourselves into the life of the Cuban people, sharing the shortages and trying to remove some of the natural distance between foreigners and Cubans.

We settled in.

Margaret wrote a 500-page book on Cuban women, a project that took eight months of traveling, doing interviews, writing, traveling again, working long hours in hotel rooms and at home. Trying to say what it was like for Cuban women before, and showing how they are living the Revolution today. Letting them speak for themselves. Probing, explaining, criticizing. . .

One thing Margaret really learned is that you can't judge the success or failure of any revolutionary process apart from what it has meant in peoples' lives, what it has meant to *them*. That sounds so simple, but I guess maybe it isn't, because a hell of a lot of people apparently would rather judge things abstractly, without historical perspective, eliminating the human factor almost entirely. How can you make any judgement about the life now, under socialism, of a woman like Haydee Mendez, without finding out what it really means that she was living under *feudalism* in the Sierra Maestra just twelve years ago? You can't. You can't begin to judge the extent of Haydee's liberation without seeing the extent of her slavery before the Revolution.

Margaret saw that Haydee, thirty-eight, represents the last generation heavily scarred by the past, whose responses and reflexes are conditioned by the real suffering of the generations before. Taking part in the new order, giving and helping to build it, but without the great transformation the younger generation grows into with the Revolution. Haydee's daughter is already a very different kind of human being. Margaret got to talk to some women doing what was traditionally "man's work" in a foundry in Matanzas. They were talking about hard work, about the prejudices against women engaging in arduous manual labor. One of the sisters held out her hands to show what the foundry work had done. "They're not beautiful hands in the old ways," she said, "but they're beautiful, communist hands."

The book reflects a struggle and a complicated process. This is a transitional period in Cuba, especially so in the case of Cuban women. While *machismo* isn't being attacked in a head-on, systematic way, the economic and social basis for the oppression of women is being removed. This makes for a very uneven process, with contradictions both in consciousness and policy—you can see the changes in the younger generation most of all. This Revolution is releasing liberating forces which leave no Cuban's life untouched. But you can't speak of "woman's status in Cuba" as if there was a single level all women are at. That's what made writing the book such a difficult task. In it, Margaret evaluates the process through which Cuban women are being liberated, as well as the forces still preventing them from developing fully. From reading the book, you can see there's no question as to which forces are winning out.

One of Margaret's intentions in writing the book was to make precisely this point, to help counteract the completely distorted, one-sided, unrealistic, and often unprincipled critiques being produced and consumed by the left in the capitalist countries.

Margaret had a kidney removed several months after arriving in Cuba, a major operation leaving a scar almost halfway round her waist. It was a powerful experience for her in basically two ways. First of all, she got to know the Revolution better. Much better and much deeper. Socialist medicine, socialist doctors, socialist nurses, socialist hospital! Taking care of people so they can make the Revolution, taking care of people because they are people and that's one of the Revolution's responsibilities. Amazing to be sick without having to worry how much it will cost! Amazing to be treated like a human being! The fantastic way the patients help each other get well. Doctors having to do their work in underdeveloped conditions, but doing a far better job than their money-hungry counterparts in the "advanced" societies.

Secondly, Margaret had to come to terms with the physical limitations having only one kidney involves. Gaining another kind of strength from dealing with that. . .

Margaret was chosen to be on the jury of the Casa de las America's literary contest in 1970, in the genre of poetry. It's the most important literary prize in the Spanish-speaking world. She spent around two weeks reading manuscripts, feeling somewhat unsure and hesitant at first about judging poetry in Spanish, something Sergio had always told her she wasn't capable of doing (despite the fact she is completely fluent, even to the point of dreaming in Spanish). Proof that she was really capable of judging poetry in Spanish is the fact that the other judges unanimously agreed with her choice of the winning manuscript, which she happened to read first. After reading *Diario del cuartel*, by Carlos Maria Gutierrez—about his prison experience in Uruguay—Margaret was convinced it would be the winning manuscript: conviction not intuition. Feeling sure of herself reading Spanish. . . undoing the brainwash of years.

When *gusanos* kidnapped eleven Cuban fishermen on the high seas in the spring of 1970, the Cuban population freaked out and held protest demonstrations day and night in front of the Swiss embassy (which inhabits the building that was the old U.S. embassy, and which represents U.S. interests in Cuba now). Margaret was asked to speak one night, representing the American people, and she had her turn at the microphone alongside Vietnamese, Laotian, Angolan, Dominican revolutionaries, from many countries. . . She spoke for just a minute, saying the most important thing, that there are Americans, especially black and brown Americans, who are fighting imperialism, growing numbers fighting the same enemy who captured the Cuban fishermen, and she expressed the fighting solidarity of the American people with the people of Cuba.

Our relationship has weathered hard struggle and ripened in it. I'm sure we haven't struggled enough, though at times it has felt as though we were hitting bottom, scraping bone. A lot of heavy changes, a lot of unmasking, ugliness and beauty. Moving forward with each redefinition of the relationship.

They've all been *political* changes, the definitions all political. What it amounts to is fighting to bring our lives—ourselves—and the principles we're fighting for in line with each other.

The stakes aren't our relationship or even ourselves as individuals, despite the fact that we are individuals and this relationship has served as the framework for so many struggles. We know that what it's all about is the Revolution. The relationship (somebody once warned me against the word). The richness of it, the poverty of it. The richness of loving and getting to know another human being. The poverty of monogamy as a forge of revolution. Trying to deal with historic contradictions.

Where does the energy come from, where do the examples come from, where do the values and ideas come from that keep pushing us further and further? Not from thin air. Not from two individuals.

Margaret got elected by her fellow workers to serve on the Book Institute's union committee, a very unusual thing to happen, since she's a foreigner. Her election seems to me all the more significant in light of the fact that the workers' movement had shortly before been revitalized and invested with a new strategic role in this phase of the Cuban Revolution. The workers at the Book Institute placed their trust in Margaret, a deep vote of political/human confidence. They wanted her to speak for them in her own voice, because they trusted that voice. They saw it was a revolutionary voice. The workers were assuming it would be their own voice.

Margaret hadn't had to shout in order for her fellow workers to hear that voice. She had to work, she had to serve the Revolution, she had to behave like a human being, take responsibility, and show discipline. But if she'd speak in that voice to me, I'd have

44

a hard time hearing it. I'd have a hard time hearing it mainly because I've been listening for another voice for so long. Because a woman isn't supposed to talk to a man that way. Because the noise of the past in our relationship, the structural interference, the background static no amount of fine tuning is going to eliminate, make it hard to listen.

Being forced to listen. To each other. Bringing home new consciousness the Revolution gives us, day by day.

Engaging in criticism and self-criticism is essential for revolutionary work. At the Book Institute, and at my work center, it's the most natural thing in the world, an organic part of the job. The collective good is always the reference point, the question "How can we do more and better work for the Revolution?" always comes first. Individual problems are tackled collectively because they affect the collective, and people are made stronger and more aware.

It's not possible to have this intense day-to-day experience, to see how it brings *results*, and at the same time be resigned to the protracted ache of a prerevolutionary relationship in another part of your life. And that's what it's all about, trying to bring the parts together. That's what I meant before when I said all the changes have been political.

It's been harder for me to bring the parts together than for Margaret, I think. Is that a fucked-up thing to say? Harder or easier aside, what I really mean is that it is taking me longer. I'm only beginning to learn from Margaret's togetherness, to learn not to tighten and resist the influence. To learn to accept leadership from her.

It goes both ways. The things I'm learning, the road I'm traveling, my advances and breakthroughs all become forces in our relationship. We make progress little by little. Sometimes it takes backsliding on one of our parts to make the thing move forward.

We've been consolidating a relationship which has helped make us better people, better revolutionaries, or else it hasn't been worth shit. To the extent we hold each other back, we're betraying the Revolution. To the extent we free each other to fight, the relationship is useful to the Revolution. The more struggling we do, the more I feel Margaret's a *sister*!

45

•

Margaret is a prolific woman. Prolific writer, hard worker, long talker. She is always involved in some project, several at the same time. Getting things done. She can't rest until the thing she's doing is done. Once she starts something, she finishes it. She is a fast worker, dependable and reluctant to say no to a request for help. She's always doing extra work, including shit work. Superfast typist. She has done interviews with a Brazilian revolutionary sister, a Cuban party member who was a maid before the Revolution, a Uruguayan journalist, American sisters and brothers. Written articles on Cuba, defending the Revolution against all kinds of attacks, putting things into perspective for people back in the States. Translating articles from the Cuban newspapers for Movement publications in Babylon. Trying to make Cuba understood to Americans, trying to help the Revolution back home. And endless diary entries, endless letters to family and friends—giving concrete information, uplifting news, support for sisters and brothers. She wrote several poems shortly after arriving in Cuba, but the poetry seems to have stopped for the present. Poetry sometimes doesn't seem big enough to contain the changes and express the messages which have become her life. The changes which demand new forms to express them. Messages looking for a new voice to shout them. Which demand direct action. And when the poems finally break from her again, that's how they'll come.

She is always talking to people. Long, intense conversations with close comrades and acquaintances alike. With groups of people. She was invited to a factory to talk to the workers on International Women's Day. Ended up listening. . . Breaking through the defenses, inhibitions, and dishonesty we carry with us from the past, to meet the even gaze of a Vietnamese brother. Reading—devouring books and newspapers from home. Helping other people in their work. Developing a critical consciousness— criticism to help and support comrades. Finding time for all of this. Job, kids, housework, loving, talking, exploring, and struggling. Fitting it in. Getting bigger to fit it all in.

NOTES FROM A DIARY / 1970–71

NOTES FROM A DIARY

From a society of consumers to a society of workers
. . . fragments of the first two years in Cuba

1970. February 24:

. . . this frame, this place, this lesson, this huge "Revolution greater than we ourselves". . .

. . . More concrete examples of how the consciousness of an entire population can be raised in a revolutionary framework: my friend Regina was coming home from work on the bus today. She was with her seven-month baby girl. The baby suddenly went cold and limp; Regina thought she was dead. Not only did the whole bus become involved, but the bus driver immediately veered off his route and drove the bus nonstop to the emergency entrance of the nearest children's hospital—about twenty blocks away. The baby's better now. . .

. . . We've seen a film worth talking about. *Los Hombres de Mal Tiempo*. Mal Tiempo was one of the decisive battles (led by Máximo Gómez) in the Cuban war of independence. The idea was to make a documentary about that battle. As the filming progressed, though, someone got the idea of visiting the old people's home in Havana, where a half dozen men close to a hundred years of age still live. They are veterans of the real battle of Mal Tiempo. They filmed the initial conversations, in the garden of the asylum. Memories. Coming back into present tense. Then they took these old men to the set. In a station wagon. You see them sitting there, *being taken,* still huddled in age, still reduced by their sedentary existence. They arrive at the set. The actors are young men, as young as their long-past youth. The takes begin, the troops, mounted on horseback, come roaring into the valley. The old men watch the reenactment of their moments of glory. They begin to explain, make suggestions, correct, show how it's done—they pick up the *machete*, pick up the rifle, one of them—Estéban Montejo, "El Cimarrón," one hundred nine years old—begins to dance, the drums, the movement. The men come alive. They move. They are totally involved in the battle; the screen battle and the battle in their collective memory are one experience. When the take is completed, the men slow down. The old men walk away, more slowly, disinflated again, again reduced to the present. But the meeting is unforgettable. The original documentary has been replaced by one that could only happen under very special circumstances. It's like the final merited tribute to these veterans of that intermediate phase of "100 years of struggle."

•

February 26:

One of the clearest things present these days: Jaime saying to me, "The Revolution needs years, not days." Of course the years are made of days, but it's important to see the thing as long range, not get dragged down by temporary illness, inability, work always toward the greatest whole unit. . .

. . . The *zafra*, the sugar harvest: every day opening the paper to see, before anything else, how the harvest is going. . . The effort is on everybody's back. . .

•

March 2:

This city. Under the paint that was there. In the streets. On the bus, looking out a window at the same height. Invariable now. I'll never see that green-and-yellow door from below, looking up. Coming to a city grown up. Eyes moving at the level of a bus window. Imagining the other side of that door, around that corner, the bus going in the opposite direction, that field *before* they built the factory. How would it have been from the beginning? Living about the boats instead of talking about the boats. Feeling the blades of grass with the soles of my feet; now I'm feeling the blades of grass through my eyes, looking from the window of the bus at the field where the blades of grass. . . It moves off. In another direction. Never running down that street, never having run from somewhere or to somewhere with someone behind *here*, always walking down that street, the rhythm of arrival. The rhythm of just arrived. . .

. . . We have a home! On Friday they notified Robert at his work, and he called me. It's on Línea between N and M, near the sea front. A ninth floor. A glassed-in terrace looks out to sea. Fresh ocean air all around. Imagining it won't be blazing hot in summer. . . Rooms and rooms, the kind of perverse luxury of the old bourgeoisie where mirrors on the outside of closet doors open to mirrors inside the same closet, chandeliers in the bathroom, etc. Indirect lighting. A service elevator and servants' quarters. But the wear of eleven years of Revolution and blockade: the kitchen stove will have to be fixed, there's no longer any hot water, one window—frame and all—is out. . . Robert, who was to have gone to the cane fields yesterday, didn't leave, and won't until we're installed. Maybe a week or two at most. We have to get our ration book, register at the local food store, etc. The children are delighted. They'll finally have a place to move around in, bring friends up. Hotel living was getting difficult. And there's Anna: to be able to live with our baby again! Making arrangements to get her into a children's circle nearby. Yesterday afternoon a plumber from the hotel offered to come over and look at the bathrooms, electrical outlets, etc. When we got to the master bedroom I pointed to a glass-enclosed wall crèche with a gold-leaf frame. "That's about the only thing in perfect shape," I said. "You know what you've got to do with that?" he laughed: "Put a picture of Che or Lenin in there. Break the spell!". . .

•

March 4:

. . . The rationing, scarcity of items available, etc., is one of the phenomena that most surely split people right down the line. Here, as in everything else, they must define themselves, and they do so unwittingly. Revolutionaries are courteous, helpful, all day long—in spite of long lines, waiting, errors, heat, exhaustion. Greed spells itself out in big letters across the faces and bodies of the dissatisfied, unincorporated types—they'll push and shove themselves over anyone in their way to buy a paper flower or a towel. Federico Alvarez put it very well today; "It's a matter of

51

criticism *vs.* self-criticism." In the consumer society there's nothing left in our everyday life but one kind of criticism or another; we can't conceive of self-criticism—in that sense—because the power isn't in our hands (yet). Here, those who are against the system, or can't understand it, criticize. The revolutionary is self-critical when the need arises, because he includes himself in the workings of the system and he knows the power is his. . .

•

March 30:

. . . It's beginning to be hot. Working in the heat. Thinking of the heat to come, much hotter than this, and thinking how I won't mind it. The energy coming through that. . .

. . . guard duty Friday night for the Defense Committee, midnight to 2:30 A.M. There's three posts: two schools and a dry cleaner, and two ten-block rounds where you call into the central zone office at regular intervals. . . very serious sense of neighborhood defense, real neighborhood control by the people.

•

April 4:

. . . Sarah's birthday party was great: Saturday afternoon. A wild magician who works for the State's consolidated magician's league, no charge, to dazzle the kids (and me). A birthday cake so huge the whole building was still eating gooey icing on Sunday night and Sarah brought a big piece to school. One hundred twenty-four soft drinks (as well as the cake) on the ration book. Lots of kids: running and inventing their own games. None of the gift-giving thing; that's pretty much disappeared here, where toys are only available at this point once a year and on an equal basis for every child under twelve. So there was no "Look, her gift was bigger or better than his," etc. . .

. . . On the bus to work this morning, I thought of a photographic essay I once saw. It was by Luc Chessex and dealt with the image of Fidel in the Cuban Revolution. Luc says there's no hero worship here, no official image propagated by the Cuban government, to make idols of its leaders. Witness instead the great number of spontaneous, "homemade" images: Fidel and Che and other

52

leaders everywhere painted by the local artist of the factory, cut from magazines and arranged on the block's Defense Committee bulletin board by the most "artistic" neighbor, traced in lights, masking tape, or typewriter x's! All over the place. . . It's true.

•

April 20–26 (the cane fields):

"El Mamey," one of the two camps belonging to the Cuban Book Institute, near the small village of Palos, in Havana province. . . Real emulation, respect for work capacity differences, exaggerated cleanliness. On the part of the women at least, making sure not only themselves but all around them bathe twice or at least once a day. . . cleaning the dorm twice daily: it's a good dorm, with two rows of double-deck beds (poles stretched with burlap and covered with a thin quiltlike mattress, three modern toilets, and three good showers in back, boxes and cord turned into night tables and clothes lines. The women: forty-four of us. We range in age from seventeen to twenty (the majority) to several older women (forty to fifty). A rough seventy-five per cent from the print shops, factories, and binderies connected with the Book Institute, the other twenty-five percent intellectual workers and secretaries: writers, researchers, style-correctors, designers, receptionists, telephone operators, etc., etc. Big mamey trees around a central clearing, cook house and dining hall, two men's dorms (approximately two hundred fifty men), one of them—the men's dorms—used to be a cockfight arena back when that was a Cuban sport, pre-Revolution. . . Relations between the two sexes very good, great comradeship, naturalness without intimacy (or very little, if it exists at all). Food very good: a typical meal consisting of white rice, meat and potatoes, fresh salad (coleslaw, tomatoes, and cucumbers), bread, fruit or dessert, at least several times a week yoghurt and another several times ice cream. Coffee at least once and usually twice a day. Some of the men (the regulars) eat with their own containers, accustomed to years of mixing everything together in a pan or can. They don't trust the metal food trays, or just feel better eating that way. . .
    . . . This morning Rolando (director of the Institute) came out to the camp, wanted to pick up one of the mill workers who was in a car accident yesterday and lost a finger, wanted to take him

in to Havana for treatment. I was again impressed on the breakfast line (I was passing out oranges, two to a person) when he
passed his oranges up. Constant consciousness among the vanguard workers and the leadership. Monday night we all listened
to Fidel's speech at the funeral of the five men who lost their
lives defending the nation against the recent mercenary attack
near Baracoa. Five of our men. The attack only one of a more or
less constant series over these past eleven years, but a big one.
Stray mercenaries still being rounded up. Modern American
weaponry. We get the Voice of America station clearly out here,
and a local Miami station as well: the lies are fantastic. They speak
of "hordes of Cuban Army going over to the side of the mercenaries, peasants joining the liberators," etc. Their objective, this
time, of course, is to damage the ten-million-ton harvest, knowing
the bulk of Cuban military is cutting cane. What they never seem
to take into consideration is the Cuban's real love for this Revolution, the fact there's a militiaman and/or woman in every
home. . . Fidel was right-on as always. We felt the passion, and
it released, to some extent, the anger in us all. There wasn't a
murmur in the woman's dorm during the speech. Absolute silence,
and Fidel's voice beating against the walls and bunks. . .
    . . . The radio is on all the time: music, black soul music while
we're peeling potatoes, the Beatles, Cuban music, Mexican songs,
an occasional song that takes me way back. The mill station
brings the hour, news, more music, whatever's necessary. There's
not much cane left here, and what there is is twisted and hard
to root out. The fields around Havana, Matanzas, Pinar del Río,
and Las Villas are coming to the end of their season. The harvest
will finish up in Oriente and Camaguey. The women here have
been piling and planting next season's cane—two very tough jobs.
Last night there was a camp meeting in which the director, Herrera,
said that in view of the fact that many of the *compañeras* have been
run down due to the heaviness of the work, they were lining up
a cutting brigade beginning today: twenty women would be able
to cut instead of pile and plant. Great cheers all around. The
women were chosen by Dalia, the woman responsible for our
dorm—according to ability, length of time at the camp, etc. . . .
Because of the kidney operation, I've been working in the kitchen:
making salad for some three hundred people twice a day, sweeping
and scrubbing down the dining room, peeling potatoes, serving

yoghurt, bread, dessert. Hard work but I've been taking it exactly as I could/can, stopping when I can't go anymore. No explanations needed. I've never felt so good in a group of people. The sun is hot. There are a fair amount of mosquitos. Some of the women have netting. A few hens and roosters peck around the camp. In the dining hall there are two good wall murals: one with Echevarria, Che, and Turcios Lima. The other is a beautiful photograph exhibition someone did of Lenin's life. A photo of Che looks down from one of the cross poles that divide the kitchen area from the dining tables. Small alternating Cuban and Vietnamese flags are strung above the tables. Yesterday they passed out cigarettes: men and women alike get three packs of mild blend or eight packs of strong mix a week, a couple of boxes of matches. We nonsmokers give our ration to the smokers. Everyone gets one roll of toilet paper a week, and there's cotton for the women, when they need it. A tiny, informative camp newspaper every day. Lots of reading, more among the factory workers (who always want to up their intellectual level) than among the intellectual workers (who want to rest their heads). . . A contingent of very young girls from one of the binderies makes it into town (nearby Palos) almost every night to go to the movies. Sometimes they walk both ways! Most of the women fall into a deep sleep around nine or ten. At five it's "On your feet, with the same enthusiasm!" to wash, out for breakfast of coffee and milk, bread or crackers, sometimes an orange or two. The women, among themselves, are generally very reserved when it comes to dressing and undressing: there's no walking or lying around naked, even in the dorm, and the few women who do so are criticized by the rest—sometimes in the form of jokes (with a good deal behind them). . . The men treat the women who work with a respect I've never seen between the sexes—they may be *machos* in their homes, but most of them here at the camp transcend their own hang-ups, and the treatment is very beautiful. Political consciousness is high among almost everyone, and a real consciousness of what people are doing here is present in everything and everyone. Once in a while we get the Voice of America on the radio: it provokes laughter more than anger. The earth is red. The horizon gentle. A few *guajiros* with their animals. A few horses. . .

. . . A fellow from one of the local radio stations was passing a

55

questionnaire around: what the cutters think of the harvest. All kinds of questions. From reading a sampling of filled-out sheets, I gained the following information: a sixty-four-year-old cutter here is averaging three hundred *arrobas* a day (an *arroba* is twenty-five pounds), a fifty-year-old cutter who has thirty-four seasons behind him is averaging five hundred daily and is one of the best in the camp (an average man working as hard as he can—or an average woman doing the same—cuts about one hundred twenty to two hundred *arrobas* a day, though there are those rare exceptions who cut twelve hundred or more). The vast majority of the cutters wash their own clothing (as opposed to sending or taking it home to wife or mother), most of them consider emulation in terms of their own capacity, they all dig listening to the radio and reading, the most common comment when asked about what they think of the coming spring rains in terms of the commitment to processing ten million tons of sugar: "*Meterle más mano* ('work harder')." A good ninety per cent are up on the regional and national harvest statistics, world news, take an active part in at least one revolutionary mass organization, and have a fairly high level of political consciousness. Doctors visit the camp approximately twice a month, though most of these men and women don't have need of frequent medical attention. . .

. . . *Thursday*: Seeing the "millionaire brigade" (a group of twenty men, repetition of such groups all around the country, who between them have cut more than a million *arrobas* of cane —they each cut an average of five hundred a day) all come in to eat at once. Incredible. These guys go out to the fields much earlier than anyone else, and they stay later. Voluntarily. They all strangely resemble one another, especially in their bodies, around the waist and thighs. They are exceptionally tall and thin, very thin, very lean in the waist and hips, with hard but absolutely unexaggerated musculature, long hair, long early Gregory Peck, Western movie faces. Beautful human beings. . .

April 29:

. . . On the bus to work early this morning I began to recognize the city, the first time that's happened, coming to the corner I

56

know, seeing the next block before it happens, not always to have to be attentive to the vaguely-known. Beginning to know. . .

. . . The *Rampa* is alive with Lenin: his presence in image and word, and the dictums are particularly apt for the daily struggle in Cuba now: that need for constant heroism in everyday work. . .

May 14:

. . . Yesterday, for the first time, I witnessed a woman afraid to go up in the elevator at the building where I work. She laughed nervously and asked the woman running the elevator if the "lawyer on the fifth floor could come down to talk to her"! Afraid of the elevator. A woman from the country. Reminding me again of what the Revolution had/has to combat. . .

May 17–20:

. . . Again, as dozens of times before, imperialism unwittingly renews the surface of the Cuban Revolution: fresh energy runs in the streets of Havana! I say surface because underneath it's a strength that needs no impetus outside itself. "But just in case they wonder," a woman in the crowd told me, "just in case they still have any doubts, this should show them where we're at!". . .

All eyes and much of the world's anger were focused on the latest U.S. aggression: Cambodia. Cuba was no exception to that indignation. The daily papers were filled with news of the invasion and stateside reaction: protest stretching now to groups previously almost unaffected, and culminating in the assassination of the six blacks in Jackson and Atlanta and the four white middle-class students in Kent, Ohio.

Most Cubans heard about the incident of the fishermen for the first time in Tuesday morning's *Granma* (morning paper, and official organ of the Cuban Communist party): U.S. imperialism, this time under the guise of the "Alfa 66 Group" of Cuban counter-revolutionaries in exile, had sunk two small fishing craft and kid- napped the eleven fishermen who made up their combined crews. No one knew where the fishermen were, but the international news services released a photo of the eleven men. They were described by A.P. and U.P.I. as "alleged prisoners." The faces all bore the calm, proud, and unafraid expression of men who know that, even fishing, they are open to constant aggression from the north. . .

. . . The news broke Tuesday morning, and by dawn Friday spontaneous crowds had begun to gather before the old American embassy building on the Havana seaside drive. It's a big glass and concrete structure, now used by the Swiss "representing U.S. interests in Cuba." As Saturday's *Granma* explained, the building was nationalized and reclaimed by the Revolutionary government through law 1121 (July 23, 1963) in answer to the U.S. arbitrarily confiscating funds from the Bank of Cuba at that time. The Swiss chose to ignore the law, however, and they have remained in the building ever since. . .

. . . It was natural that the offensive building should draw the people's protest; the crowds grew, people began coming from every sector and every part of the island: fishermen, peasants, workers, teachers, professional people, students, cane-cutters, army militia, artists, doctors, housewives, and small children. The long vigil began. But far from a "silent" vigil, this was a loud, strong demand: WE WANT THE RETURN OF OUR BROTHERS! NIXON, WE DEMAND THE RETURN OF OUR BROTHERS! By Friday night there were fifteen thousand people before the ominous embassy building. And concentrations began taking place in Camaguey, Oriente, Isle of Pines, all over the country. By Sunday the crowd in Havana was two hundred thousand. . .

By Saturday it was clear the protest was there to stay; more than one placard announced WE'LL REMAIN TILL THE RETURN OF OUR FISHERMEN! All over Havana flags and signs went up, from balconies and windows spontaneous expressions of the people's solidarity and rage: SON OF A BITCH NIXON . . . NIXON IS THE HITLER OF OUR ERA. . . IMPERIALISTS OUT OF CAMBODIA AND VIETNAM. . . WE WON'T TRADE HONEST WORKERS FOR MERCENARY WORMS (referring to rumors that the U.S. wanted to trade the fishermen for the captured mercenary soldiers being held here since the April invasion at Baracoa). Flags and tents all over the protest site. . .

Defense Committee and militia teams manage the huge masses of people; they've had years of experience and do their job perfectly. Petty irritation, impatience, or resentment have no part in the order of the crowd; a calm, a logic, and a serenity underlie the tremendous strength and power of the demonstration. (Bruce Jacobs said: "It's not really a demonstration, but a mobilization"; and he's right). Revolutionary order isn't imposed like the raucus order of a capitalist state, and it isn't received in the same way either. Rest rooms have been set up as well as a hospital tent; food and coffee are distributed free. Soldiers with hand radios roam the protest site, maintaining constant contact with what has by this time become another facet of the world situation. A speaker's stand has been set up, and people begin coming spontaneously from all sectors of the population, as well as Vietnamese, Cambodians, Laotians, Africans, and other Latin Americans who want to show their solidarity with the Cuban fishermen and the Cuban Revolution. . . Cuban painters channel their anger onto huge panels set up and painted by them at the protest site. Cuban musicians play and sing all the time. . .

Everyone seems to be in that area before the embassy, and yet everyone is also working, everyone is on his or her job, everyone is vigilant, everyone is on sharp guard, life and work go on as usual, the ten-million-ton harvest moves toward its eighth million. . .

. . . Some of the fishermen's families are here, from their village of Caibarién; one of the mothers speaks to the crowd. Manuel Ascunce Domenech's mother speaks too: her son was hanged by counterrevolutionaries in the fall of 1960, during the great literacy campaign. He was teaching an old peasant man to read and write; both of them were tortured and then assassinated. . .

Saturday: . . . the street was blocked off this morning and the bus I take to work couldn't get to the usual bus stop—I ran to the corner as it came off Línea and up M: the driver stopped short and opened the front door. "I didn't realize they had that block roped off," he said, smiling, "or I would have stopped at the corner." Solidarity everywhere. . .

. . . Walking through the crowd again tonight, suddenly threw my arms around a woman I'd seen the night before and had a warm feeling about, a woman from the Federation of Cuban Women who had been with the fishermen's families. "It's like the first years," she said. "Whatever happened, whenever a new revolutionary law was passed, whenever something important

59

happened, the people responded like this. The nationalization of the big foreign companies, mid-1960, we made big coffins I remember, and we buried General Electric and Socony Oil all night long. The next morning everyone went to work. Just like now. It's bringing back those years. . ."

. . . *COMANDANTE EN JEFE: ORDENE* (COMMANDER IN CHIEF: WE'RE WAITING FOR YOUR ORDER). Spelled out everywhere. How to explain that outside the context of this Revolution? "People wouldn't understand," said Laurette Sejourne, standing beside me and looking up at one of the banners. "They even use that as some example of blind faith. They don't want to see it; they can't see it. . ." And it means, simply, *here we are, present, ready and willing to follow the orders of the man who led us to victory. . .*

. . . Monday the rumors begin: the fishermen have been freed! They've been taken to a small island in the Bahamas. . . we've got to go and get them. . . foreign news services including France Presse. . . the International Red Cross will act as intermediary. . . rumors. The hymns and combat songs are interspersed with bongo drums now, kids are running and dancing through the streets. The site of the mobilization is teeming with people. THE FISHERMEN ARE ALIVE! OUR BROTHERS ARE ALIVE! The waiting becomes more intense. . . It's been more than eighty hours now. . .

Late Tuesday night: The fishermen freed, or more accurately: liberated by the Cubans. Witness the battle of strength and intelligence waged by these people. . .

A day like any other today. To work early—around seven—then to see Robert at the hospital (hepatitis denying him this experience), to a meeting with a representative of the party at the Book Institute concerning an aspect of the book about women. Thinking all the time of how we must all help to keep the production up, in spite of the jubilation. Quickly home at noon to change into pants for what I thought would be the long hours of sharing the fishermen's return and Fidel's words. I was heading out toward 23rd and Malecón, where our work place was to meet and march together to the protest site, when I found out they'd been looking for me to check in some six blocks farther down the seaside drive. They'd tried to reach me at work. All the speakers at Sunday night's rally (where I spoke for North American revo-

60

lutionaries) were invited to go out to the airport with the fishermen's families and meet the small plane bringing them in from Nassau; and all of us were invited to be present at the speaker's stand later when Fidel would talk.

Out to the airport—Rancho Boyeros, outside Havana—the streets were already thick with people. Flags, placards, the exhortations and dictums changed now, and some of the signs said VICTORY. . . WELCOME HOME FISHERMEN. . . NIXON? . . . WE'VE WON ONE MORE BATTLE IN THE LONG STRUGGLE WHICH IS OUR REVOLUTION. I've never seen so many people, but more impressive and harder to describe than the numbers I've never seen *such* people: the qualities of dignity, authenticity, and consciousness coming through again and again like waves beating and beating the senses. People who remembered it, said "This is second only to Fidel coming into Havana in January 1959!" The fishermen's families are simple people, sea people, hard people used to a certain kind of life and a certain known risk. In the spacious waiting room we moved through together two hours before the plane came down, they talked and opened themselves to us—and to newsmen and television reporters, interviewers· from the film industry, and journalists from other sectors of the national press. One of the wives, the most verbal: "They didn't give us back our men; we *took* them back!" Another: "We wouldn't have traded them for miserable traitors for anything in the world!" "How does my friend here feel? Well, she hasn't slept, eaten, or lived for nine days either—just like me." "My husband used to own his own boat, we ate everything he earned. He joined the cooperative right after it was started. Yes, now we've got a home, everything, thanks to the Revolution. . ." "Her? No, she's not my daughter. She's another one of the wives: fifteen and with one child already. What? Yes, I have four. . ." A good many of the eleven wives, twenty-two mothers and fathers, and forty-six children had come from Caibarién.

When the plane landed we all formed a double line to the door. Fidel had been waiting in a room nearby; his excitement and impatience were all over him. The secret service men holding the line in order were almost gentle; everyone wanted to be close to the fishermen. When the plane door opened they came out, and the cheers were from both sides. Some were smoking cigars, fresh work clothes had been sent them to come home in, they were unshaven and visibly haggard: nine days in hostage at the hands of imperialism. Quickly they were lifted onto the shoulders of the crowd. People hugged and kissed them, each other, people cried, people cursed and shouted. A steady rhythm of bongos came from the airport crowd. Even the toughest women, dry-eyed when they thought their husbands dead, began to cry. One of the youngest threw herself in a chair—back in the waiting room—and sobbed out the frustration of these past two weeks.

The caravan back to town was dizzy. . . Literally thousands of citizens lined the highway in carts, cars, on foot, in wheelchairs, a slow line of tractors with whole families moved slowly in to the left of the main line of traffic. . .

. . . The tribunal set up before the dead embassy building now faced a half million people. I noticed a placard that said: TURN THE EMBASSY INTO A HOSPITAL. Above the speaker's stand were the words: IMPOSSIBLE TO CONQUER THE WILL OF THE PEOPLE. . .

The fishermen began telling their story. One after another they spoke to the crowd, how they felt, their fears, their fury, their desperation and joy. "Sure, lots of food, but what did we want with food. . . ?" And then Fidel moved to the mike. He began by explaining the process by which the fishermen had been located, spoke of responsibility and of international strategy, revealed the tensions and final checkmate of these past days, and finally detailed the battle won by the Cuban people: their self-discipline, their courage, and their enormous will. As usual, he came down hard in exactly the right places. Left at that, it would easily have been one of his most important speeches, a lesson on all kinds of fronts.

But he didn't leave it at that. He might have wanted to have left it at that, he said he hadn't meant to move away from the gladness and meaning in this battle won, and I believe that's true. But he moved by ear, by heart as well as by head, as he always does, and there was something else he had to tell the Cuban people: the ten million tons of sugar, which is the current super-human struggle of a whole nation and an absolute challenge inside and outside Cuba, will not be achieved. How it was to say that. How it was to explain the reasons why—some mistakes in planning and numerous mechanical and industrial difficulties finally im-possible to overcome. How it was to deal with that, openly,

62

before and with the people: a concrete situation dealt with in a concrete and completely honest way, nothing to hide. How it was to talk about the use imperialism will make of this news. And the attitude we must have up against that. Tearing the guts from success—in that particular and unbelievably tought battle which ninety per cent of the island is still waging and will be waging till the last cane comes down—tearing optimism off to make room for a collective facing up to reality, and at the same time cautioning against defeatism. I was three or four feet from his face, his eyes, and I felt the weight of those words. The weight and the struggle in every word. . .

Half a million people were as silent as they'd been during the memorial service after Che's assassination (many people made that comparison, later). Half a million people had tears in their eyes as they shouted their support of this man who is without doubt the most brilliant, the most courageous, and most humane leader of our or any time. He said, "I hope this is the last time I'll ever have to say anything like this. . ." The people's tears were a mixture of sorrow, rage, relief, shame, understanding, and an even higher consciousness. . .

•

May 20:

The streets are heavy this morning. People on the bus are silent. The unreachable ten million tons, the news Fidel broke—it's saddened people, fucked them, shocked them. But, as Mayda says, it's a natural shock, it has to take its toll and time, and these people will come up again strong, tomorrow, the next day. . .

•

June 5:

. . . Peru has just suffered (these past days) one of the worst natural catastrophes in Latin America in recent years: a series of earthquakes which took thirty thousand lives and left four hundred thousand wounded and homeless. Whole towns wiped off the face of the land. Cuba—with her very limited resources and possibilities—was the first country to send aid. So far several planes have gone to the site of the tragedy: the first with our country's entire plasma reserve as well as epidemic-prevention

63

medicines, the second with our Minister of Public Health as well as more supplies. A huge drive here among the people, to replace the blood donated: one hundred thousand donors! The words on the new posters: THE BLOOD OF PERU IS THE BLOOD OF OUR AMERICA. . .

. . . This morning: women always on that familiar street corner, in bright pants and shirts, hair pulled back under a variety of scarves, waiting to load into trucks and go out for a day of productive work in the fields. Every day I see the same women. Men on other corners. Lots of groups. . . .

•

June 23:

Ximena: "In Mexico everyone's white and in Cuba lots of people are black. Since I've been here, I'm already mulatto. . ."

•

June 27:

Sarah looked at a copy of *Newsweek* with a photo of an antiwar demonstration. She said: "Look, they publish these pictures so people will think they're good. . ." And this afternoon, after seeing the film *79 Springs*, she said: "I want to die like Ho— of old age."

•

July 10:

On a month's license from work, in order to participate as one of the judges in the *Casa de las Américas* literary contest this year. In the poetry category. Reading one hundred ninety-four full-length manuscripts, along with the other four judges: Ernesto Cardenal from Nicaragua, Roque Dalton from El Salvador, Washington Delgado of Peru, and Cuba's Cintio Vitier. . .

Two experiences yesterday brought me closer to the Cubans in their Revolution in a way I hadn't experienced before: the first was going to the old Partagas factory, near the *capitolio*. Visiting the factory is interesting in itself: the men and women who make cigars by hand, a tradition that used to pass from father to son and which is now largely handled by regular schools set up by the Revolution, the men and women who run the machines which produce four thousand-plus a day (the best, working by hand, turn out a bit more than fifty), the heat and that particular damp pungent smell, the nature of these people who truly belong to a *gremio*. . . Representatives from the party and the Communist Youth showed us around, talking with the workers. But there was an added dimension yesterday: the reader (that able dramatist who reads novels, stories, poetry, political material over a mike as the others work) had been reading Rodolfo Walsh's *Operation Massacre*. And Walsh is one of the *Casa* judges. The reader was just about in the middle of the book. Some of the workers had read the book through on their own, everyone had heard at least half. So, with the author present, they took advantage of the chance to discuss it. They pulled chairs up for us in the big main hall, several hundred workers— men and women—continued to cut and fold and press and roll the leaves into different kinds of cigars, as they listened, as they talked. Walsh, from the reader's chair, gave a simple but effective summary of the situation in Argentina, how he came to write the book, where the workers' struggle in his country is at now and how it compares to what happened in Cuba. The first questions were asked by the more outstanding workers: party representative, advanced workers, etc. Each—if a man—got up from his bench, put on his shirt, and went up to the reader's platform to express his question. Although the workers seemed to be more or less evenly divided between men and women, more women questioned Walsh than men. And the questions were fantastic: "Is such and such a character in the book really a revolutionary, or is he more or less acting without really acute political consciousness in such and such a situation. . . ?" "What's the relationship between the workers' and students' movements in Argentina?". . .

The second experience took place after dinner when we went to a session of the people's court. . . This particular night of trials was in a neighborhood fairly near mine. Courts composed of three judges chosen by the people from their zone committee investigate and judge civil cases which don't fall within the category of the heavier criminal cases. On this particular evening and in this particular place—crowded with neighbors, filled with benches and chairs, hung with a few colonial paintings and headed by a slightly raised platform and desk behind which the three judges took their seats—two groups of judges alternated: when one worked out front, the other group was out deliberating a case. The cases ranged from two "entrance into another's property" to a young doctor who disobeyed a militiaman's orders and entered with his small child into a hospital area which the public health ordinance has made off-limits for children. There was a case where one woman had called another "a prostitute," etc., and came to blows over a supposed incident in which the other woman had been kissed by her husband. Defamation of a mass organization also entered into one of the cases. The court clearly made exhaustive investigations in each case. Solutions were not dependent—ever—on the clear-cut facts of the case, but included the implications, the whole social context, the reasons, the *real reasons*, bringing these people here. Disciplinary action ran from public admonition to required bettering of formal education, although these courts can order privation of liberty for up to six months. In one case, pointing out the tremendous exodus of people from the country to the city, from the provinces where they are often working and living in fairly good conditions to the capital where they find living quarters a problem, the court *suggested* the couple in question return to Oriente where the woman's family has a large home and both had work. (The woman had entered an empty room here in the city, doesn't work but her husband does, and they both claimed they have nowhere to live. They had never bothered to inquire through his job—where dormitory arrangements are possible at the very least, as they are through all work places—but instead had used this somewhat dramatic way to try to get the Revolution to "solve their problem.") The court, in this case, not only explained the problems of this exodus, but pointed out the tendency toward individual solution rather than the collective solution that this couple desired. The court suggested Oriente but made clear it couldn't nor would it force the couple to live in any part of the island it didn't want to live in. These people were clearly *Lumpen*. The others were mostly working-class people who, in one way or another, and with varying degrees of education and possibility, were putting themselves at the mercy of the people's court—the dignity and sobriety was tremendous. People's backgrounds were always brought into the picture, and lauded where necessary: the young doctor, who had served in Algiers, the porter who in twenty years of service had never had a stain on his record. Revolutionary attitudes manifest in a hundred ways. In one group of judges, two were women and one was a man. In the other group, the ratio was reversed. At least two of the women and one man were brilliant. I knew that it wasn't a matter of six cases having been heard and resolved; six very serious lessons had been learned by everyone in the room. The court broke up around two A.M. . . .

•

July 22:

Two bottles of rum, one of *aguardiente*, two of cider, three of red wine, six packages of hard candy, four boxes of chocolates, six different kinds of *turon*, one small can of Bulgarian baked beans, six cans of deviled ham, one large tin of cookies, one jar of mayonnaise salad spread, half a pound of black beans, twelve pounds of pork: that's the list of extra goodies for a family of six (ours) this *carnaval* month! A real treat in terms of the usual nourishing but not often varied diet. Cost: $38.00. . .

Carnaval: All over the city, along the *malecón*, homemade decorations on every street, on every house, on every building, people painting: pictures, photos of the martyrs of Moncada, flags, streets with their own personalities, neighborhoods—you can almost tell what kind of people live in them, from the decorations. And at night: the drinking and dancing and the costumes. . .

•

October 1:

. . . The assemblies at every work place, making the new laws, revising, questioning everything, reevaluating everything, every work place up in arms, assemblies into the night, yesterday, today, tomorrow. Pacheco here tonight with 100° fever, still working, going out to Madruga afterward to study; an open truck below the window as I write this, filled with dozens of young men and women, a furious rhythm band in front of the Communist Youth house. . .

•

October 11:

Sarah started crying at lunch today when Gregory—talking about some animal or other—said several times: "It's useful to mankind. . ." "To mankind, to mankind, always to mankind," screamed Sarah. "Why isn't it useful to mankind and womankind?" "O.K.," said Gregory right away, "useful to humanity as a whole." But she wouldn't accept that. She wanted women in there too, specific and certain. . .

·

October 16:

The agricultural and animal fair at the *Pavillón* is terrific! Took the children tonight. Each display (bees, cows, trees, fruits, pigs, etc., etc., etc.) has a very sensitive and knowledgeable student standing by ready to help children (and adults!) understand everything about whatever is being displayed—the children saw movies of cows being born regularly and by Caesarean section, learned how artificial insemination is done, took model animals apart and put them together again. . . it was really sensational! I've never seen such interest on the part of those doing the explaining, nor such thorough knowledge. The whole sexual thing was approached the only way it should be: fully. And the students always encouraged the children to do it themselves, as many times as they wanted, to really *know* what happens, to ask all the questions they had. There were microscopes and a thousand things to see and use. All to folk music on the loudspeakers all up and down 23rd Street. And animals ruminating in the stalls along "N," tractors and other huge farm machines on the street closed off down to the *Rampa*. . .

·

October 19:

Yesterday, on the living room floor, little Annie pulled open Sarah's cunt, and Sarah called in to the kitchen: "Mommy, Annie's inseminating me!"

·

November 6:

After a memorial tribute to Marighella at the *Casa de las Américas*: It's suddenly turned cold. Well: cold is a relative thing, but cold for Havana—winter. And the air is great and big again, particles exist, the ocean is fierce; yesterday I spent some time looking down on it from our balcony window: it came thundering in on itself again and again, hard waves hitting the low stone wall of the *malecón*, thundering. A different color now. Last night, walking out alone into the darkness, I saw the spray immense as it hit the coast and filled the sky. . .

•

November 22:

I'm every day confronted by the different growth the children experience here, in short: how communist they're becoming! Tonight Robert and a woman he was talking to and Gregory got into a conversation about suicide, and Robert asked Gregory why he imagined some people commit suicide. Gregory immediately said it was because of the pressures put on them by a distorted or transitional society, the contradictions people face in their lives provoked by a faulty system which exploits them. He's ten. And he immediately saw it as a *social* problem. As a child (and not only as a child, but fairly recently, as well), I would have said first off that it was due to some personal problem: love, illness, etc.

•

November 26:

A statistic: for each U.S. citizen there's 1.2 kilos of waste per day. For every Cuban there's only 0.35 kilos. That's a telling blockade statistic: no wrappings, no containers, everything re-used, re-used, re-used. . .

•

1971. January 12:

. . . the union board meeting yesterday and today, meetings frequent now to pass on the best orientations to the workers: the hardship of the lack of electricity (one of the big turbines has been destroyed. . .), how the distribution of consumer goods will be handled through the work places (the first allotment is one refrigerator every two hundred workers, one television set per fifty-two workers, one pressure cooker every seven woman workers, one woman's watch per every six woman workers, one men's watch per every forty male workers, one pocket watch per each one hundred twenty male workers, one electric blender for every one hundred twenty workers, etc., etc.). These items will be distributed by a commission voted on by the masses, that is, the commission will do the investigating and make suggestions as to whom should receive the items. The workers themselves will have the final say in each case, in open assembly. Anyone wishing to apply for an item fills out a form, listing need, etc. The goods will be distributed first on need, second on revolutionary and work attitudes (assuming the need in two cases is judged to be the same), and lastly (if it still seems to be a tie) on how long the worker has been at the work place. . .

•

May 6:

. . . At the corner grocery store a couple of mornings ago, the police came and arrested the manager: "He's a member of the party!" someone said. "Better be sure of what you're doing!" "We're sure," was the answer, and they were. The pig had been cheating customers on rice, on meat, on everything. . . This is the people's justice, developing in this way at a steady pace and on all levels since Fidel's 26th of July speech last year: the people refusing to allow that medium-level new bourgeoisie threat accumulating their privilege off the rest of the people. . . ! The Revolution is taking its seat—that's the way Macías put it, when we talked the other day: now there's reason to expect a National Plenary of the C.T.C., even a congress of the Cuban Communist party (so long awaited, and the absence of which has been so absurdly criticized by some). The cultural policy has been defined, and a whole process is being unleashed, and it all fits together. It's a very beautiful and exciting thing to watch, and even more beautiful to participate in. . .

. . . *Mother's Day:* There's one gift per ration book in the stores, a choice between embroidered slippers, a housecoat, perfume, two bottles of liqueur, a set of plastic glasses, etc., etc., etc., etc. On the buses there's some complaining by the perverbial *gusanos:* "What if there are two or more "mothers" in a family, on one book?" "Then there's only one gift!" someone shouted. "What about the mothers in Vietnam? In Laos? In Africa? Do you think *they'll* be getting Mother's Day gifts?". . .

•

May 18:

. . . Gregory is *so* fantastically creative: the puppets he is making are so beautiful! (Months in which they've let him apprentice on Saturdays, with the comrades from the National Puppet Theater.) He saws the masks from cigar boxes with a child's tool kit saw, and has to save all the tiny nails, rebend them straight, and use them over again in the masks—*everything*, the simplest materials, are almost impossible to get here of course, and his imagination is always working toward how and where to find bits and scraps of material: rope for the hair, what to use for dye, how to apply paint and how to *invent* that paint, using tiny Vietnamese flags for eyes on one of the puppets, an outgrown dress of Annie's for the body. His masks have the purity of Africa, the imagination of ten year olds, and the courage of Revolution in them. . .

•

May 22:

I was telling Sarah about my sister and her husband having problems and perhaps separating, and I told her that her little cousin Jeff was feeling sad and confused these days. She sat down and wrote him the following letter:

> May 21, 1971
> Year of Productivity
>
> Dear Jeff:
>
> I know how you must feel Jeff, I went through
> the same thing when my mommy and my daddy were
> separated but your mother will probably get
> married again and you'll be happy like before.
> I felt like you do when my mother fought with
> my father. It'll pass.
>
> Sarah

71

June 19:

. . . It was great at Gregory's school today. Just being in the Social Circle for Scholarship Students, "Comandante Cristino Naranjo" gives you a lot to think about: this used to be the Havana Sports Casino; it's literally lined with deep red marble (exploitation, Italian style). There are all kinds of sports facilities, restaurant, huge hall for dances, theater, swimming pool, dressing rooms and showers, beach, tennis courts, etc., etc. The live-in students at the sports school where Gregory goes work out here. Sitting in one of the big rockers along each side of the huge hall where student dances are now held, I thought of what this place must have been like before the Revolution. They say there was a small runway where private planes landed twice a day direct from Miami. Now elementary and junior high school students—all colors, and from all parts of the island—sit on the sundeck or walk arm in arm, run, laugh, eat sandwiches and drink root beer at the long bar. . . One of the workers, serving at this bar, was telling a group of students: "I got a job here because I was a pretty well-known boxer, featherweight; but I'm tellin ya, there weren't many blacks walked through that door. . .!" He gestured to the main entrance, above which a photograph of Cristino Naranjo—wild long hair, beatutiful face, rebel army fatigues—looked out at the group of young students. Today I was in that hall waiting for the end-of-year ceremony to begin: a simple affair held in the small theater. Gregory, as the Pioneer leader of the school, gave the report on the year's activities. And he ended his report: ". . . as communists, conscious of our ideal, we will. . . " And all the students voices joined him in responding: ". . . be like Che!"

June 26:

. . . In a long (eight to seven) workers' assembly yesterday, we discussed all the comrades' merits and demerits, and proposed, discussed, and voted from among our ranks for the growth of the "Vanguard Workers Movement." It was the most profound and combative assembly we've had: people learning to really search

72

each other out, in the healthiest ways. I was moved and happy to be elected Vanguard Worker. Of the twenty-one workers in our collective, nine of us were elected. . .

·

June 27:

We took the kids out to the huge new Lenin Park, forty *caballerías* (a *caballería* is thirty-three and a third acres) of beautiful lush green rolling land: little cafés, an amphitheater built into the rock facing a stage floating on a small man-made lake, rodeo and corral where people can ride beautiful horses, an aquarium, library, art gallery, amusement and infant areas—everything. A lot of it isn't finished yet, some of the main things are open, and more will be inaugurated on July 26th. We decided to take the train ride: it's a petroleum-run open-air train that makes a run of some twenty kilometers around the park site, and it takes forty-five minutes. As we drove up, the train was just getting ready to pull out; the ticket booth was closed, and there were maybe ten or twenty people like us, waiting on the platform. There was a slight hitch while a couple of militiamen pulled a couple of young guys and a girl off the train. They weren't treating them brutally at all, just insisting and pushing them gently when they kept resisting. Apparently, from what we gathered as the thing continued, these people had provoked a fight in the ticket line, which they continued on board the train. One of the guys threatened to knife one of the militiamen. The militiamen were working at the train site, aiding the smooth running of the new operation. It was clear they were real people's soldiers. The guys disturbing were told they couldn't ride on the train. They got angrier and angrier. A couple of people—the *gusano*-types who, while in the extreme minority, always seem to be around to take advantage of these kinds of situations—began shouting things about "people in uniform," etc. And then a whole lot of people in the crowd burst forward in that totally Cuban verbal/action way and just defended the militiamen and everything they stood for, from their immediate action in this case on up through the country they represent. It was so beautiful! One guy who came through the loudest and very right-on just kept saying over and over:

73

"Go on with this military *vs.* civilian stuff, go on with it, military *vs.* civilian *shit*: just look at the *facts* man, the *facts*—you guys were creating trouble; these guys are protecting *the people.* . . !" That's where it's at. . .

On the train (we took the next ride, after being helped into line by these same militiamen, and after being given free tickets for each member of the family) we rode close to a great couple with a twelve-year-old son. The woman began telling me about her other child, a daughter who's already fifteen and has a boy friend. "She's probably waiting for us now," she said, "in the portal of our house. . ." Then she went on to talk about her house: ". . . big, with three bedrooms and a telephone; we've lived there eleven years. . ." The husband, who works for the telephone company, said they'd been coming to Lenin Park since it opened. As the train advanced along the track, he pointed to cafeterias, restaurants, the corral, the amphitheater, etc., as if they were really his (which of course they are!). When we passed the library he said: "There are lots of tables and chairs, even out under the trees, and you can just go and take a book and *read* it!" At one point, passing some barely adequate housing, Robert said it looked like they didn't have electricity. At that the man got pretty indignant and answered immediately: "They have electricity; around here everyone has electricity!" There were two young women dressed in bright green cotton dresses. One of them leaned out off the platform connecting the cars at one spot to receive a big bouquet of wild flowers from a comrade waiting by the track. She shared it with her sister hostess. Farther along, the workers at a local factory were lined up outside waving to the occupants of the little train. . . Actually, the people in those houses did have electricity. . .

This morning I was thinking about what kind of a society makes people trust other people and also feel about themselves that they are *like others* instead of different, special, superior, unique in a variety of untrue ways, etc. The traditions of racism, "rugged individualism," private property relations and worth by ownership, etc.: all those root things in the North American culture (not the real hidden culture, but the camouflaging capitalist-system-as-culture) set people apart from each other. I've never —until recently, and I'm just beginning—really thought others

74

could do things I knew how to do as well as I can do them, never trusted others completely, always assumed responsibility for *everything* that I cared at all about. It was always hard for me to trust others to be able to do these things. I always thought I was the best driver, writer, typist, cook, etc. Lover, poet, thinker . . . When? Wow! Now I'm beginning to feel—though it's a process that's been taking place all along, ever since coming here —that I'm just like everyone else, and everyone else is just like me—potentially. I mean it's not the old "everyone is created equal" thing; I really believe it. I find myself *acting* on it. . .

•

July 26:

Fidel's July 26th speech just ended; it's just after nine P.M. It began at six-twenty—Fidel talked a lot about this past year: the accomplishments, the results of the new methodology, the new policy traced precisely one year ago on last July 26th. Almost *all* areas of production are up: tremendous effort and especially a new and more rigorous organization had raised production from ten per cent (light industry in general, with some products much higher) to over fifty per cent in certain areas! I felt that increase as my own, as *our* own, the only possible way to feel it in this kind of society! And of course Fidel talked about problems—he never shirks that responsibility. The terrible drought (especially affecting the Pinar del Río tobacco harvest), the fact that further progress in certain areas will only be possible with a degree of technification very difficult to attain in Cuba's present state of development, the continued blockade (cases of certain countries pressured into refusing to buy any products made with Cuban nickel, etc.), and the African swine fever detected among Cuban pigs. We've all been very much aware of the fact that this plague hit Cuba just a month before the yearly and longed-for extra pork ration was due the people for the 26th of July; sabotage has been in all our heads since the epidemic broke out. Fidel said they have yet to come to a conclusion about the cause of the epidemic. There are similar epidemics in other countries, especially underdeveloped countries. It may have been coincidence; it may have been an enemy plant: only further investigation will tell. Fidel mentioned that one of the first focal points detected had been near Rancho Boyeros airport, which bears keeping in mind; but true to the absolutely revolutionary honesty which characterizes this government, there was no attempt to play the possibility of sabotage up, or .propagandize that without being sure. Instead, Fidel used the opportunity to reiterate the need for better safety and hygiene methods, in all areas of animal breeding and slaughter. . .

•

July 30:

One summer like this one I went to San Francisco. That was about thirteen or fourteen years ago. Another summer I was heavy with Gregory growing in my belly: 1960. Sarah was born in April, Ximena in June. It was summer when I drove those long hot hours to Guatemala and back, summer when Robert and I swam at the house in Acapulco. It's already been two years since the agent entered our home one July 7th and the repression began for us in Mexico. Two years. The children have been here in Cuba two years. Today I felt like writing another autobiography, another one like that feverish sixty pages while hidden in Mexico, calling it "Autobiography Number Two" or "Second Autobiography"—I even thought: maybe I'll want to write another four or five years from now, and another going through menopause, or another when my children are grown. Another in another country. On another front. Happier or more alone. It would be interesting to compare "autobiographies" written by the same person—even treating the same events as they get paler and paler—at different times in her or his life. . .

They'd be different. Different eyes. I think the autobiography I'd write now would be fleshier, more precise but more jagged, the incisions deeper, there'd be less scar tissue to camouflage the wounds. More open. . .

. . . *Torrential* (the word) seems like it was invented for island rains—they pour and beat and slash against buildings, people, the water rises up in the streets nine floors below, carrying sticks, sand, bits of wood, toward the *malecón*, the sea. . . And the waves gray and mountainous, rising up in the sheets of gray wet-

ness. . . The thunder cracks as if it were inside your head, a volley
of lightning shooting through black clouds. . .

•

October 6:

. . . George Jackson is dead, and thirty-eight are dead at Attica,
and others are dead across the country (U.S.A.), and Lamarca
is dead in Brazil—Adamaris's vibrating revolutionary passion and
energy this morning in an interview, talking about Lamarca;
she worked with him, was imprisoned and tortured and finally
released into exile when the Japanese consul was kidnapped—
and day after tomorrow Che will be dead four years in America
though alive in all of us, multiplied hundreds of thousands of
times symbolically and actually in everything we do and want to
do and will do. . .

. . . Our Defense Committee needed three blood donations to
honor Che's death this year, and I volunteered: spent one whole
morning at the blood bank (yesterday) with Joannie and Ambrosio.
Ambrosio was the only one who actually got to give, as Joannie
was rejected for being one pound under the minimum weight
limit (one hundred ten pounds), and I was rejected for having
only one kidney. That was sad. But the blood bank was a beautiful
sight; for that alone it was worth the morning lost to work. The
place was filled with literally hundreds of women, men, young
women with babies—small babies—on their laps, old people who
must have just come within the fifty-nine-year-old upper age
limit, all different kinds of people with beautiful faces, the faces
of people who just matter-of-factly give their blood now as a
revolutionary duty, every three months if they can, while they
can, through the C.D.R., through the work place, on special
campaigns like the Peruvian earthquake (when one hundred
thousand donations were collected in ten days!), always ready
to give this part of themselves the Revolution has taught them
is needed. . .

I thought of the U.S. blood banks I remember from the days
when I was giving blood in New York, selling my blood for five
dollars on the mercantile market, along with all the downtrodden
of the big city slums: junkies, the poor of every color, everyone

doing that sale for another meal, to pay the rent, to make ends meet somehow in the rat race. . .

. . . In an ice-cream line on Sunday (new neighborhood ice-creameries springing up now, taking the pressure off the mammoth thousand person *Copelia*, and shortening the lines all over to ten or fifteen minutes), an older man heard me calling Gregory and started up a conversation, asking Gregory when his birthday is, because his name was Gregory too, talking about the "Saint's Day," etc., etc. Obviously a religious person, or at least a believer. Gregory knocked me out by very courteously but firmly telling the man: "I hope you don't try to get your children to believe in saints and God and stuff like that, because for the children of the future, God's going to be ancient history!". . .

•

1972. January 22:

. . . For the first time I had the chance to go out to *Alamar*, where seventy-six of the thirty-three-man "microbrigades" are working on "building their own houses." It's been almost a year since Fidel's beautiful plan went into effect: the definitive answer to this country's housing problem (the Revolution's greatest single problem, without a doubt). All over the city, at the end of one street, on a previously vacant lot along another, the housing is going up. All over the country, too. The microbrigadists can be distinguished by their white construction helmets with the *Tupamaro* symbol on the front. Wherever they go, people greet them, are happy! But in the Havana area, *Alamar* is the largest single project. It was begun before the Revolution: the typical middle-class housing project on the outskirts of an expanding city. Construction was interrupted by the triumph of the rebellion. A year ago, work started again. . .

. . . In a given work place (factory, office, study center, farm) a microbrigade of workers is chosen because of specific skills. Maybe some of them are carpenters, or one knows something about electricity. The other workers commit themselves to keeping the production level up to standard. The brigade workers have never built anything before. They become construction workers as they go. A brigade from one factory or work place takes on a whole building—four or five stories high, an average of twenty-four apartments per building—and under the supervision of one or two experts construct to D.E.S.A. standards! As the men "build their own houses" they become a new skilled labor force for the Revolution. They learn everything from reading the plans to finishing touches. The furniture shop will make all furnishings for all the units, which will be given complete with telephone, refrigerator, gas stove, and television. . .

. . . Eating *merienda* (crackers and *malta*) one of the workers told me: "I thought I was just going to carry out one more task the Revolution asked of me. . . get some experience in leadership, when they told me to come out here. I was a mechanic at that factory over there. . . I thought this was going to be like going to the cane fields or something. . . But we didn't even know how to read plans! Now we're construction workers! We're building our homes, but we have a new job skill too!"

Eventually upward of eight thousand families will occupy the houses already planned. The first buildings will be given out on February 25th, to mark the first anniversary of the project. The workers give the building over to their work center, and in a workers' assembly the masses decide who will get each apartment. Then the worker chosen will pay six per cent of her or his salary regardless of whether or not others in the nucleus are wage earners! This is the temporary rent—until the nation can abolish rents altogether. . .

•

January 25:

. . . The *"plan jaba"* (shopping-bag plan) went into effect at our grocery store a few days ago, and I used it yesterday for the first time! Robert brought our bag in the morning, with the ration book, and around six I went to pick it up. Filled! No more lines, no more waiting, no more hassle for working women! Actually, the plan is for all families where all adults are either working or studying. It was started in Matanzas almost two years ago, and is now all over the country (Havana being the last place to be incorporated—in line with Cuba's emphasis on the countryside, Havana is always the last place to be touched by revolutionary change, since in pre-Revolution days it was the typical central city sucking off the provinces). . .

. . . *Time* is always the big problem in revolution—money? When visitors come I'm always brought up short by the formalities again: "Who's taking whom out to dinner. . . who's going to pay. . . etc." We don't even *think* of money here. The minimum wage earner makes enough to take his whole family out to a luxury restaurant a couple of times a month. Most people have surplus cash. Basic necessities are so cheap, or they're free like hospitalization, education, funerals, "pay" phone calls, sports and other recreational events. . . So it's time that precious. The continual improvement in distribution, food buying, restaurant reservations, vacation plans, services: that's what people look for and share in bringing about. The *"plan jaba's"* my best news this week!

PART OF THE SOLUTION

EVERYONE COMES TO A LIGHTED HOUSE

Last night I had a dream in which with my own hands
I picked up fat fresh mushrooms
and sliced them into a frying pan.
I watched them shrink and brown
and tasted the delicate meat drippings, fat, and the
	thin browned mushroom slices
together in gravy.
My dream.
The first one, the first moment I've had
in which mushrooms didn't feel terror in my body.
In the same dream there was a funeral parlor, dark hallways,
	a family,
prominently a son. Showing us the way.
High fences at night.
Gates in the fences, made of the same wire.
Gregory, Sarah, Ximena, Anna, Robert and I
walking as fast as we could, not running but walking
through the gates, from gate to gate, along the fences,
	through the night
away from the funeral parlor toward
a lighted house.
The faint smell of the mushroom gravy brought us to
	the kitchen.
I have been three months in Cuba
from the year of decisive effort to the year of ten
	million tons,
from effort to sugar,
				economy,
people moving together and if you don't move you're out,
	away, somewhere else.
Fidel's "Within the Revolution everything;
	outside the Revolution nothing"
isn't the private property of intellectuals.
It's just like breathing.

Everyone comes to the party.
Imperial humor dried up, lost: "What if they gave a war and
    no one came?"
Just 'it always being very simple, my Vietnamese friend
    who said
"Before the Americans it was the French for a hundred years
    and before that
the Chinese for a thousand. And now the Americans.
    We *know* what slavery is."
Very simple and all the time
people moving together.
I'm moving.
I look at the worried letter from my friend in the States.
    I try to read it.
But I'm moving.
Out of my dream.

NEW EYES

It was a large well organized meeting, we sat
with wooden file boxes on our laps.
Knees loosely together the moving bus jogs them
and faces turn between them, the faces of men, terrible
    fast memory
of those mad brown eyes accusing
You're showing yourself again!
An other tempo concern, floating in and out and between
these fibers of real. Yes. Now is another matter
even in dreams.
In this one it was a meeting, we had come from
    somewhere else,
conspiracy, running, the dark interiors of old Ford coupés,
the smell and touch of the semivelvet seats
rasping:

The file box is suddenly full of secret compartments
doors that slide this way and lift, that way and close
over another space
and messages in them all.
One says *I am the one who was there before. The same one.*
A girl stands up and says *in America even dolls give dolls*
as presents.
It's the nature of capitalism I say *to condition the need. . .*
but suddenly I see her face.
He's carrying a gun.
Escape. Among all the gifts. Get out.
Far away they are raising their hands and arguing,
discussing the words.
The dream went on but I woke up.
The bus is full my stop's coming up everyone has new eyes

THE RITUAL, ANTONIONI

I
Like Blaise Cendrars, thinking I am a bad poet
because afraid to go all the way,
afraid, no, seeing
all the way not coming to me.

That third figure in all the photos
man in the emptiness between the other two, silent
because unseen
exploding on the radar screen.

All the lines, gestures, action
shoved into the rest of them, crumbling
on crowded space.
How we go, no, stay
on the bus from compromise, the wheel
turns
direction becomes inverse to singing candles, detail
blurs out the forms come on
one by one
separate and moving
all over this single face of shame.

II
Antonioni spreads it out, the tender light
denied by men, one and another

castrated with indifference
shrugged with acceptable sun
and the others keep on moving through, sand,
no class distinction here:
all in the same closed wagon.

And the little boy
moving the wand, opening out:
that part of us which sees through closed eyes
and open hand
those colors charge through space, possess it,
white for a sterile death
red for the stumbling sense
factory equals house equals ten equals wall:
water for possibility.

III
And I, only letting it trickle in,
removed one space from imposing projection
remember this room
sitting before this screen, rows,
and waiting outside, the people,
getting up finally and waiting outside.
The pains coming regular now
the movement near
expelling another small gift /inverse/
containing all the world
and those with us, the time later the words:
"all her life she will carry with her
our eyes, our ears" all her life
she will bear us with her step
but by her angle on the sand.

Going all the way now, you coming,
you moving in,
you ready?

In loose circles and endless strings
around and out from St. Paul
and Minneapolis Minnesota
those country rows of houses
grow toward everywhere America.
The great white map this web of peaked roofs
and ample lawn rakings
of fall leaves fences dividing subtracting
cars in and out more cars in than out
and the great white happy proud and peaceful
in-between America
stamped by every windowpane by every standard heating
air conditioned welcome matted
birdbath glow-ball lawn.

Out in front down to the stretching road
close by the proud and private path
next to the shiny individual mailbox
there is a special private individual newspaper tube
a very separate place sometimes two or three
or up to ten very separate private places
where every morning a newspaper is stuffed
or every afternoon
depending on publication time
or even more than one newspaper
one newspaper for every holder
for every separate private stamped and indexed
newspaper clotch. crotch. crack. hole.
newsprint cunt.

And every morning or every afternoon
like clockwork accurate and american
a fine young man a fine young american youth
breaking out in the business world

not hawking on street corners from have-to
but riding his bicycle or perhaps his late model
motor scooter motorcycle american or maybe german
or dutch
in any case this fine young motorized man
thrusts his rolled up string tied compact
fresh american newspaper bundle
into that waiting upright american individual slot
presses his hot off the press bright new news
into that tunnel
and closes the tiny swinging individual door
and throws the shiny perfect individual lock.
The news safe the people safe the lawns safe
the young and old men reassured
the cunt closed.
The ride goes on the next box and the next
the motorized ride continues
down endless webs of country roads
the stuffing and closing the fine young american boy
is learning how to stuff the news of his country
into the waiting holes of his country.

He rides and rides
his work will never stop
the houses stretch out the boxes wait
the web grows bigger and bigger
the freshly painted individual mailbox newsprint
receiving line
goes on and on
but the fine young american boy
never gets tired
he rides forever
a natural replacement of Irving's horseman and
as headless

MINNEAPOLIS/ST. PAUL—10/24/65

WEDDING POEM FOR DIANE

—for Diane Wakoski

Your father George Washington has finally given you away
—finally, as is repeated to you, given you in marriage,
the cream-colored sacrament. Upright

as all our fathers claim
this act is mainly horizontal. Its movements
taking you by that surprise or laying you out
in willingness removed and related
in the same space. More than natural boundary lines
requirements or armies of invisible parents
more than the children we create or come to be.
Much more than numbers signs or borrowed litanies
the objects of retreat
this act is gift and age balanced out in space.
Somewhere

between moon and sun
somewhere on playgrounds
by untouchable telephone booths or under the heavy
        black eaves
of heavy black buildings
your bodies have become permanently horizontal,
his penis, all his tools,
your heart-shaped face and angled hand gestures
have become sideways.
horizontal.
down to each other.
into.
beneath.
through grass domes and cloud drift.
My hands laying on toe
a gift by which to sing
a poem by which to offer
another touch of horizontal hands.

NEW YORK—10/21/65

THE DECISION

Shame
is not a common denominator.
Some take it heads up
or a bird lying across the knee.
I remember

how will it feel when we go back
to that place,
memory being so much a part of the game,
and I say

the bird, those pictures
you showed me,
the definition we give to them, the line
we draw between.

Help. me. become.
All those places have their names
and I have mine.

MOTHER OF THE YEAR

Through all those matching teacups ladled out
the spiced cinnamon
corsets corsages
or united effort. That is,
people getting together,
the blizzard of '42

or dry tornado,
veined cushion repeating itself
rising
and falling under crepe, taffeta, the knit suit,
the children mustn't know
or do

except at funerals
what we read in the papers
birthday conversation with the pastor,
jim crow, indian chief.
My tumor. As big. As a grapefruit.

Even the fruit of a variety
thick-skinned, sugar added
to the bitter juices. Safe.

Once a year she takes everything out, lines the drawers,
newspaper smelling of cedar, lysol,
look at that goddam yellow face over there
killing our boys!

HUMPTY DUMPTY

There is light
on the edges of those words
taken apart
            we cannot put them together again
as they said of the men, the horses, that fat egg-shaped king
who sat on the wall and fell

(or was pushed)
down
the cycle begins again now
of these acts, places to be, having been, it is
Bolivar, San Martín, Martí,
America

moving out of her skin
                        stretching,
stretching to light
and where there is light there is
fire
    sky
        sun
            profile
of hands.
Moving, going beyond the wall
and the fat man who fell
the pieces of words in sun
become

plain weight of the scales, that's all.

NEW MEXICO / A Song

Reies Tijerina they had to get you this time
with eighty tanks they had to take you out
the fist
          it shakes in our faces now, but someday. . .
they had to take you out
of those mountains
Sierra Maestra in the uncle's own land, but

Fidel was beaten too
at Moncada, there's time

when the wind circles round
comes back

to slap them in the face.

USING THE SAME WORDS

I wanted to tell you
everything,
the first places the long times made of silence the parks
trees crowded together the light between them
disappearing, going out like old sirens, the air
after being broken
where the streets come together
I wanted to tell you stroking and stroking my hair
you listened.

I wanted to talk about men, repetition,
the uncontrollable tremor between the legs

and children
the long-taking leave begun in ecstasy, put your hand here,
I wanted to say
places dates names pieces of mirror
and stencils of history
knowing you heard beneath the words the other music
running along inside
you listened.

I said
surrounded by water, an island, now,
these words have gone back
recovered original form
                          tense
                                place
the absolute center.

If I ate nothing for five days it was because air,
revolution, the earth beyond and under my feet,
I needed nothing but that.
God knows if you understood. You listened.

AUTHORITY, OR THE AUTOPSY OF LOVE

—for Rita Siegel

When they had me in six years old
it was just a praying mantis stained on the seat of my
        blue jeans
(what we called them then)
and furtive wash, in the bathroom
my hands remembered the five-dollar fine
a conversation turned to jail in my head.
Authority made accident a possibility, hard put,

the hands remembering, washed, erased
where I sat down

already they had me twenty-five years later
American Embassy Mexico City
no questions but a certain knowledge
plans bigger than either, the safety belt
tight
throttled
that same authority, it's a fear born

bred and built-in
comes with a do-it-yourself ointment
for the nervous rash,
garbage to sit in while you wait.

Afterwards,
always afterwards reason separates the pieces,
claims the lock on the door came in your Christmas stocking
can't keep out or let in   .
that's for the dark blue or berry red come to take you by
    the hand

when they had me in love
it was something else till it ended
or the shadow fell against all gravity and now
you have it in both hands
by the pins and belts it is closed between fingers
and it doesn't seem to matter that you read

:made in China
smuggled out through Hong Kong

and counterfeit.

THE DEAD PHOENIX

—for Ana and Agustí Bartra

Tonight a wishbone cracks in my throat, the sun
cursed into blackness,
tonight I would cry
                    gravel and blood harpoons
on my country, still my country
:refusing to let you go though the papers changed hands
though circumstance found me here or there
or fat or aging, still
you sit on my eyes a sick and spreading fruit
stinking through rotten skin
with hands with long green arms
great fungus on the world—
Oh tonight I would cut your wrists with a terrible love
between my legs
I would drain you and fill your veins
embalming thirty years of tender faith, that act,
and watch you sink and know
no god you trust

HISTORY

Who is not my lover
who is not my lover
                    age, that taste
in the mouth
not my lover the big stick that moves, my brothers,
close in your distance, hovering,
the wind, even in this room, makes a map of my face,
recruits the forces of skin
                              rice
                                   whiplash
golden eyes that are not my lovers

here in this bed

SO MANY ROOMS HAS A HOUSE BUT ONE
ROOF / 1968

first trip to Cuba
for my compañeros

I
The gray interior comes alive
and burns, it is
a natural quickening
what you see with the eye, touch,

the hand runs over it, picks up,
the fingers ache or curl
under
(I remember not being able to sleep, the moon
crying in my mouth, half open, the current
jolting and jolting our bodies)

this landscape hurts
as it shows me everything is real, everything
equal to its own weight
to touch it touches off the pain inside
:those who stay at home have never left
but those who go do not arrive, only here

it is different, this circle too
is fire, burns,
makes the measured breath impossible.

Oh, it is all one, together, it is all divided, open,
never to be repeated, always to be eaten,
swallowed whole.

II
flocks of birds before our windshield, fast,
dipping together to become earth and lifting

to be birds again.
surely they are swallows, color of the spotty shoulder, earth,
Chihuahua pampa land.

You said the world those words touch
needs sight of swallows
but I see the birds themselves
in need of what I write,

as some unclassified event.

III
I have held off in all things, response being slow in me
to come, lift its head,
yes, I have waited

against the movement of my hands
while filling space with dancing feet,
wise shoulders, socky eye and ears
with premature death in them.

I have been child,
lover, wife, mother,
even aged and all the roles converging,
playing upon themselves in me

left open
        salty
                half, or
overdrawn in pieces, being
all of them and never only one.

At thirty I go unwilling into girdles, painful
coming whole.

IV
If we can create a new language for this, a new
place,
the way a house crumbles
on all its walls, the way
the armed farmer who killed his unfaithful wife with a knife
when asked why not the gun said
No, my gun is to protect Cuba
                                    /create
a new language for this, we must, the old
is swollen
:foreskin with no place to go.

V
In that place Moncada, the farmhouse
where they met the night before
took an old couple to carnival or the party
for a fifteen-year-old girl.

The barracks, the photos, the uniforms
heavy with blood, they were
crazy,
crazy and clean, one hundred and forty

men against moloch,
against all it is necessary to be against
and more than half suffered the fat hand
there at Moncada, suffered

and died.
The other half grew six years

101

labored in birth, came through,
the sun wiping blood from its eyes, stretching
its wide mouth in song.

VI
Che lived in that shack, what's left,
one year in this mountain, he has gone,
and others. Fidel
further up, high jungle

once covered all of them
who fought, made a history
from weeds, scrap iron, the blasphemy
of knowing how
and won.

They opened this place, took the trees
from the ground
bulldozers laid bare red clay.
Six thousand went up this year

to sleep in hammocks, hang tin cups
from their belts,
will be teachers, six thousand
in the Sierra Maestra
and eight years thinking what he said
:the odds were against us then,
two hundred to one.

VII

One side a surface where the hole forms, opens,
to persist means look through
or change
as water runs over the found object.

Here
I circle, my hand becomes still, steady,
my skin not as white as it was,
the sun burns

slowly.

It is the body being washed
where even will removes from need, where the limb
cracks, reaches the climax of day,
cracking and cracking

against its own face.

Here
someone says
:that child or this field
laid down by a new hand is climbing
the almost lost straight of my back as it turns
I stand still, moving
in this open space
I am touched by skin
no longer wet, distilled

or trembling.

VIII
No one knows why the first man came
or stayed, settled
this land where the sea moves away from nets,
where heat

hangs in the air, turns swamp to dust
and calls it jungle.

Between the coffee plant and palm, removed
from all Cuba,
no water (cut Guantanamo's pipeline then
and let it run) no road

till the Revolution hung cement, Sierra de Cristal,
pushed a highway to the sea
(18 times the money raised, they say, and 18 times
was spent),
spit out the yellow tar that clogs your teeth.

What brings years to your houses, I look
at your face and you can only say
:water,
he who drinks the water of Baracoa
does not leave, a smile,
But there was no water, I say,

only now there is water and pale windscraped houses
motionless
and streets erased in leaf, foam, a birthday,
in the street I take someone's hand, it is offered, think
:here too the Revolution is

a plan, an explanation,
here no one knows why they stayed
but they did.

IX
Turning his face to one side and up, out,
that many years framed in sugar.
Here it means

juices, the cutting, hand again and once more
around the knife,
defense,
sun over nature as it breaks
                              with men
against so many miles of coast-
line.

From the beginning to end which is much more
than bread of every day.

X
Like Alice, having passed the glass
to the other side, hands left
with the rupture, shreds of crystal, splinters,
here

on this one
we are only 90 miles
(from home? off shore?)
It is the function of the glass, that shore
no longer home, we find ourselves

on this one, claim it, eat
                              breathe, work
in context, look in the glass of our own hand, see
:man equals come equals fill equals
live
    love
the structure of the poem.

XI

At the level of arches, columns
framed in mahogany, pieces of sky,
a gull floats,
moves his wide wings towards poets, we

are sitting with cut glass, the colors of sea,
these blues and greens invade,
belong to us

as once belonged to Dupont or (as I prefer to think)
never belonged but built by him, preparing
for a change of colors
he refused,
could not have held in hand or eye.

Dupont built this fortress of a house,
a wide gull floats beside the cupola, Dupont
prepared the golf course
where egrets and wild hens nest
and poets walk. We sit,
it is different now.
Dupont was mason, paid the help, drank
daiquiris
but the gull turned, the change came brute

and sure.
Dupont fled this peninsula and died
and poets sit, keep company
with this gull
stayed with Revolution on his wing.

XII
The eight-year-old profile says
:here, I will show you,
and it's not even eight if you count

the invasion, cyclone in '63,
having to invent, everything, subversion
and blockade.

The profile of eight years
shows articulate lips, eyes with music in them,
strong teeth,
settles over the island

like the words of a poem
catching up with themselves.

THE STONE

I'm searching for a word in English, not in Spanish,
and even in English I can't find it. I can't remember
the name given that smooth object
that fit in my hand.

I can feel the entire surface of my hand
around it, the heat coming
from it still, the matrix,
the veins, the surface
even after the fact, even after

I left the smooth stone on the beach
and when I came back the next day it was gone.
Can you understand? It had gone.
Whether by its own power or taken
I don't know

but I know it was my talisman,
that's the word, it was mine
even if you said
"If it's really yours it will be there," still
it was not there
but it *is* mine. I hold its heat.

THE DYING GRANDFATHER WHERE THERE WAS NO LOVE

I don't know if he's dead yet.
Maybe he died a few days ago, the mail
takes so long. I don't know.

He almost died Wednesday morning my father said
and then rallied, then
went out again
but not completely. Hearing my father's voice

saying mother went 2,000 miles
to give a dying man blood, *her* father.
The useless wait the useless words, consoling,
maybe even real.

I don't deny the possibility.
I don't deny the probability, somewhere, perhaps
someone must care, perhaps
his wife. After all.

I only wonder that my own emotion
is nowhere past the curious
question
and answer. That far apart.
That dead.

THE BLACK, MARKET

I

Thirty hours time moving away. A magnifying glass on what surrounds. Situation opening like a wound. It begins with a car door, opening over and over again behind my eyes. The car stops. Violations we commit every day. Every hour or every minute. Of every day. Again the car door opens, slowly, the boy and the bicycle coming. Soundlessly against the door. Silently falling. Spreading out. The boy's pants are caught in the chain. There is blood. The boy's leg is not straight. It is turned. The boy's brother is crying.

People coming nearer. This is the center. People coming, they are all around me now. SPLIT, GO ON, GET AWAY, GET OUT. You can leave now. You can go away. You can close the car door and drive. You know the rules. In Mexico you know how it is. You can leave. Possibility.

Choice. I open the door and get out. I try to tear the pants away from the chain. The boy's brother is crying. The boy doesn't speak. I am not here. In the post office I call an ambulance. Outside there are more people. The boy has been moved to the curb. The waiting begins. Inside the thirty hours time has a different body. The ambulance doesn't come. The police.

II

Eight years ago in New York someone said
:Everything is getting more instead of less.

Exaggeration. At the precinct there are faces. Watch chains and bellies. Eyes gone dead still going in skin. The frames. The boy is taken away. What's left is

First conversation   How I say he is not my son he is
my son but my other sons are sons this is a bad son who
insults his mother and no ed-u-ca-shun he who I admit my
son is a shit to be talking like that who aint never been
taught
        yes
            you see I admit
it
is this terrible life the problems ay the suffering

He is locked up. She leaves. Her arms crossed. He is locked
away. I am sitting in a chair. There are a hundred people
in this room. There are five spitoons under the gray desk. I
sit on a chair and remember how you liked Kafka in my head.

Second conversation   The body was found face down
the latrine these are his clothes not much
Go ahead
pick them off the floor he is
only your son

The mortician has a small face he plays with his hands watch
chain he waits for the body. The man and the woman sit on
a bench. Beside each other without touching. She is crying
his silence betrays him. It is only their son. Was.

Third conversation   Come on we aint got all day
don't look at the floor come on tell me what happened
girl
so you went to the hotel
permission your mother didn't give
you were out all night
and what happened next
what did he do to you how many times
did you like it huh did you
many times

111

Sixteen years old. She liked it. Fine. Silence. What young
people will. What they like these days. I am sitting on a chair.
It isn't my turn. Yet.

Fourth conversation   O.K. STOP. SEE ANYONE YOU
    KNOW
IN THIS ROOM? no no no I don't know no one but
    uuuhhhy
you
Moves forward two fingers held up
for a smoke
I saw you I know you why do they have me here
I was walking when my friend was shot I don't know
beside him his eyes began to blur

The doctor who picked them up in his Mercedes-Benz is being
held. Connection. Invention. Face.

Fifth conversation   Always people like you
to bother
But what did you do to my dogs
                        COME ON WE DON'T
                        HAVE
ALL DAY
WHAT'S YOUR
BEEF
First I could ask who you are. . .
TAKE HIM AWAY!

III
I will make a statement. Yes. He will write it down. I will
tell him what happened. I will make the mistake. Thinking.
He is a human being. I have forgotten.

The boy has been taken to a hospital. In this room time moves on the other side of a door. There are friends. They bring coffee. And cigarettes. The phone is in use. The boy's family appears, they are poor, they have faces. We talk. The condition of children. Having. Theirs. Mine. The insurance adjuster. A boxer. The Bronx and a yellow jacket. His nose not surrounded by face but he has to say. It's all right. The coverage is medical.

It's all right the injuries. The boy. He has fractured his leg in two places. Someone has been to the hospital. The family says it's all right. Only that. The mother looks at me from her eyes that are still alive. I want nothing else from you. I want to say I want nothing else from you. But no one lets her say it. To listen is not part of the process. Kafka across the floor curled up against the walls in every corner. The machine is not to be stopped.

IV
In the morning they take me to the tombs. The objects are taken away. Parts of the body bleeding out in the watch the earrings the blanket. In the large room there are three cells. The heavy barred gates are open. But the green door is closed. The lock is the size of both my fists. Together. It is morgue cold. The crappers are full. If it weren't so cold the stench would seize my head. It is seizing my head. Each cell has four cement slabs. Two on the bottom. Two on the top. In the first cell four women are sitting. I walk to the second and sit on a slab. I get up and examine this room. There is a shower and a sink. I sit again. And walk. And sit. In the corner there is a broom. I sweep. It is the moving back and forth. To grab hold of time with my hands. One of the women comes to me where I am. Come talk to us she says.

First woman   Ay madre mía santísima I have been here
12 days
they left the bags in my house
how was I to know and six months pregnant
the food none of us has eaten
beans and a roll at one o'clock
Today I am going to speak

Second woman   Do you know anything about
     my mother
I wonder about my canaries
On Saturday I killed my father the reporters
     always coming
it's that drug they gave me the witches
Being here I am cold my mother you know how she is
since Saturday no one has come they are all against me

You see through that window the birds could fly
At any time I could attack
and do.
My mother.
My birds.
Saturday.
Not.
Here.

Third woman   Sixteen days it's no joke
they pay 50 pesos to talk through the screen
and five to send food in
I didn't take the clothes
it was all a put-up job
this is no joke. No money. No lawyer.

Fourth woman   Rubs her leg and watches me pee

114

V

Thirty hours. I am cold. This room is real. The stench is eating my brain. If I sleep here tonight I will go mad. No. What is this but a window open on the real. World. Yes. I will go mad. No. I will get out. No. I will stay. Forever. Only a matter of time. Yes. I will go mad. No. It is not real. I am cold. Fifteen minutes have passed. Two hours. The sound of the lock the sound of the heavy door. The jailer brings a package for someone else. Leaves. The hand the voice goes out. No one is there. Four women beneath the surface of the earth. Five women. Cold. Hands. Time. Broom. Shit. The broken window. Wall on the other side. To be able to tell if the sun if the sky if the hour. Moving. If the world.

The door opening. This time it is for me. I walk out up the stairs across the courtyard the people waiting their faces their hands the way they stand. This time it is for me. At four o'clock I would be taken to the penitentiary. On the other side of the room I see my friends. Look at their faces. Asking. The boy's mother. The boy's uncle. You, Maru and Felipe and Sergio and Eduardo. Eduardo your hands the gesture of finish. All right. I am taken to a desk. Where I sit in a chair. I will make another statement. But the judge is making it for me he is making my statement for me he is saying the truth I told is not the truth he is making another truth. A better truth. I am free.
Free.
At liberty.
To go.

VI
Eduardo
:Let me tell you what happened he said. I called my uncle on the phone. I haven't seen him in years. A hundred people wait-

ing in the office. Pieces of paper in their hands. I was taken past them into the inner room. Mr. Canudas they said. The engineer. To see the lawyer. The boss. Let me tell you how it felt. Of course it was a mistake he said. Glad to do it. Don't mention it. I have the power. The power. Quite all right. Glad to be of service. Any time. I have the power.

VII
Walking out I begin to count the hours. Move back. Become time again. I am free. Completely free. The four women will rot in that cell. Forever. They do not have a friend who has an uncle. Only a system that teaches the crime. The word justice. Lives nowhere.

2/7/68

THE DREAM / 2

In his dream he was at the end of a long hall.
Was it a dark hall?
At the other end of the hall he saw the nude figure of his father
bent over an object he could not define
moving up and down.
He began to walk down the hall, walk
towards his father.
As he came closer he saw
his father was pumping up and down up and down
working with a bicycle pump
blowing something up.
Arriving he saw his father was pumping
a gooney woman she got bigger and bigger

116

and his father kept pumping
up and down
and the woman filling with air
got bigger and bigger
and was his mother.

As he watched his father kept pumping
and the woman's legs his mother's legs
filling with air began to rise
and separate
and suddenly
from between her legs the pumping air
filled the head of a child
coming out
from between her legs a child emerged.
Was it his brother

When the dream was over
after he had told the dream
he realized the child's head
was his.

SAD POEM

My eyes are rimmed in green, surrounded by green frames
when closed
that's the color I see out of the black
and it makes me think of Joel's Little Green
or the green of those cold hills in my childhood dream
(the one with the lonely archway and halls and the four men
playing cards in the building I knew was a madhouse,
    repeated)

117

Green means tired pain.
Green
used for grass, traditionally used for food, growing things,
green fields, green season of the year,
verges on yellow now and circles my closed eyes
spinning, propelling
the ache deep in the center of my skull.

It is the opposite of the bodyless red we saw together,
        formless,
with no name but red
in the heat of happily closed eyes.
The happiness has left with the red, they have gone
        away together
in order to come back.

The green now is only a place (not that word
you hate, but a definite physical place)
corrosion of the wound on one side,
new baby growing after all these years on the other.

THE FATHER POEM

My father sold pipes and tobacco, a small shop
in downtown New York
when I was six I helped him
mix the blends   I remember the smell
in our basement
ending in unimportant bankruptcy.
Before that when a young man
he swept ticker tape on the stock exchange
with a broom   I'm not sure that's really true
later sold men's clothing at Lord & Taylor's and
after that

was a music teacher in the Albuquerque Public Schools.
All his life he was a 'cellist.

Your father has a hardware store
where he shouldn't in Harlem   He finds
excuses to give you money
you have no trouble taking.   And your father
is a chiropodist he owes you money as difficult as that.
And yours cuts dresses in the Garment District
but owns his own home
making Revolution more difficult
but that's the way things are
in America.
The fathers of people at any given time,
and close to me.

I have always had trouble writing about my father
and have always had the need to do so.
My father is not George Washington
but then I'm not Diane Wakoski.
My father is not Karl Marx either, he is not Che,
I am my father's daughter
waiting around the eyes   around the mouth
I am his shamefully proud jewish daughter
his daughter
the one who didn't finsh college who never
did anything according to the rules but was
a target for love, for pride.

I have always wanted to write my father's fingers
on the strings   My father's ear
close to the instrument's neck
I have always wanted to write about my father
and my mother
but my mother's voice is too complex,
too close to the mirror.

(Untitled)

Ximena has a stuffed animal she takes everywhere.
She named it

FATHER ELEPHANT & SON

then she changed the name to

EYES.

SARITA'S SONG

"Water mango, sky mango
don't cry blue celestial palm tree,
now that you've given me
water mango, sky mango. . ."

THE TWO SECRETS

I
The intentionally bald friend said it was a beautful day. It's a
beautiful day. Giant sculptures are going up along the freeway
which has been renamed Friendship Way for the Olympics.
Most of the sculptures are ugly. The country is incredibly
beautiful. The perspective is strange, going out of focus at
times. I'm sitting in the back of the car. The friend and his
wife are sitting in front. It's a beautiful day. To bury a child.
How can a day be beautiful or not—to bury a child? We're
in a hurry. We're hurrying.

The cemetery is enormous. We buy daisies at the gate. Hurrying, we are driving up, up, through narrow lanes between the graves. My mind wanders off into the collection of strange architectural objects which are not statement but pieces, arbitrary and staged. It's like a giant stage set with no play. It's so large, it goes on and on, suddenly I remember I have never been in a cemetery before. Wanting to avoid that.

The day is brilliant. I think we're going to fall off the edge of the earth. Where is the funeral? A horde of little boys running after the car, shouting Water, Water! Where is the little girl's funeral? The boys point up the hill. Up there, that's where it was. Who? An "angelito." When? Three days ago. No, that's the wrong one. Today. Today. We keep driving.

Finally we see the cars. A group of people standing together. We stop the car and walk towards them, looking at their faces in the distance, their heads and bodies, trying to recognize them. We don't see anyone we know. This isn't it. Yes, yes, it is. It is. Out of the differently dressed bodies—the bodies dressed in the appropriate funeral garb, the black dress and black lace mantilla, the bodies dressed otherwise, like ours, the men in suits, a few children—out of these bodies and faces recognition sets in: there are Paco and Chole, there is the child's teacher, who is also my own child's teacher, there is Fernanda and there is Lola. We walk to the edge of the group and stand, silent.

The only sound is the earth being shoveled. Five or six diggers are working, covering, the earth is being shoveled, heaped, the last connection is being broken, the child is being really buried. Whatever ceremony there was is over. There is no sound of crying, only the grim, twisted, wet faces, and the shoveling. The sound of the shovels hitting the earth and the earth hitting the earth. When the men finish a friend steps forward with some flowers. And another. Then a mother leads a child, her hand covering the child's hand as more flowers are placed. Piled on. A slick-suited funeral-parlor type carries a large display of flowers from a spot a few feet away to the fresh mound of earth. And another. And another.

Sometimes I went off in a dream. Sometimes I turned my head and looked from face to face. The tears, I could only feel them inside my face. And my nose kept running. I turned my face once and for the first time I saw Marcia, the mother, to my left. She was pale and distant. A small shabbily uniformed man with a cap, like a tiny lottery salesman, held a piece of paper in his hand. When the flowers surrounded the grave and the people shifted their weight in the loneliness of that hilltop, the little man walked over to Marcia with the piece of paper. He said something and her face was intent, concentrated on understanding those words. Trying to understand.

The little man stuck a small black cross with a white card in the fresh earth. The people began moving away, following Marcia down the hill. I dropped my daisies at the edge of the grave and moved off, following. Now I could see the father, Branley, the handsome actor, the elegant movie star, his arm around his wife's shoulders. He is like hurt stone. I think, this is the first time I have seen a face without expression. A face beyond expression.

At the bottom of the small hill everyone stops. We have been walking between, over, through other fresh graves. This is the edge of that huge cemetery, the new edge, the extension. There is a line of black cars, muted and shining at the same time. Five or six. The mother stops and turns and leans against one of the cars. Exhaustion. She looks up at the people coming towards her. Coming and coming. Silently a line forms to her left and one by one the people approach. I watch the line move, the people one by one hugging the mother and crying, hugging and saying the few words, necessary, senseless, prepared in desperation, an attempt at comfort, the one thing we do not have in our hands to give. I put my arms around the father who is standing before me. I'm sorry, I say. He does not let go of my hand. Finally, I have to move away, taking my hand from his, gently.

I put my arms around Marcia. She says, Finally we couldn't prevent it Margaret. After all, we couldn't prevent it.

II

Two months ago, the child was playing in her sixth-floor apartment. Celia. Celita. Five years old. Not even. The friend playing with her crashed to the pavement below. The child ran screaming to her mother. My friend!

The child retreated. Inside she kept the secret. Did her friend fall, was she pushed, did she jump? Was it a pact, for two? One side still owing? Was it beautiful to fly?

The mother took the child to a psychiatrist. She stayed with her, she never left her alone. Not ever. Because the child talked about jumping. But she would forget. She would have new playmates and forget. It was a terrible tragedy. What to say? They began looking for another apartment, on the ground floor.

In school the teacher took the tragedy into account. Celita was invited to visit a different schoolmate each afternoon. Diversion. She was a sweet child, she played well. She was very generous. She seemed happy. The mother and father kept looking for a new apartment. On the ground floor.

She said she was going to jump out the window, like her friend. No, no, don't say that, don't think about it. Forget. Did we tell her wrong? Did we confuse her perspective, trying to soften—avoid—the confrontation? Should we have tried to provoke another kind of confrontation? And the psychiatrist? He had said she needn't come back. Everything would work itself out. Everything would be all right. What did we do wrong? What didn't we do?

Yesterday at five-thirty Celita was playing in the house. Her mother and father were with her, her two brothers were there, and the maid. And a small friend, a new playmate. All the windows were secured with wire, twisted around and around to hold them shut. Tight. Except for the window in Branley's studio; the children never played in there. They hadn't found another apartment yet.

In that moment she had been waiting for, in that instant the eyes were turned, she crashed to the pavement below. Had climbed on a chair to do it. Taking both secrets with her.

THE BOY WITH THE MAYAN FACE

—for Ann Quin

Here, lifted by the comforts we despise and the incredible beauty of this place—separated by these things, as it were— you say you're going to write a story about the Boy with the Mayan Face. I'll write it too, I think, from where my eyes, throat, go back to him. It's as if it won't be possible to write or speak of anything until that's set straight, giving every detail of the encounter. You'll connect it with Bob's experience, you say, being buried in the hot heavy sand, as he told it to you, that tremendous weight. And the heat. I'll only tell it as I remember it, from beginning to end.

If you think of it, if you seek them out, you find them, you see them—many such faces—it's the remnants of a race powerful enough to have lived at Palenque, complete enough to have invented Zero. They die along the surface we work now, and we see them, they're here, they exist before our eyes and bring us up short at times like albinos at county fairs. But this wasn't a chance encounter. Or at least not in that direction. He came. He sought us out.

It was up a small embankment along the highway to Acapulco, exactly eight kilometers south of Chilpancingo, dusty dry afternoon, six o'clock when the car started going bad and we suffered its last limping energies up before the shack where the sign—on the road—said "Servicio Mecanico." The mechanic wasn't there. His wife looked at her son and the son said "I'll fix it." He looked ten. Later we learned he was fifteen. He knew a great deal about cars though he couldn't, in fact, fix this one. A thin young man wandering past stopped and helped. He held the tools; later he held the light. This place was called Petaquillas, Guerrero. Across the highway was a bus stop, a three-walled structure painted bright pink on the inside. At another shack, nearer the highway and down a few feet from the mechanic's house, a group of men were gathered. There were two dogs and, at one point, a few goats.

That was all. The road curved back towards Chilpancingo behind us, Iguala behind us, the Canyon del Zopolote—canyon of vultures—behind us and the mountains hiding Ameyaltepec, Mexica, Mezcala: those villages where Pedro—Felix in that other story of mine—killed the man who bothered his wife and where the men drink and slander their saints in the church every year and where everyone now paints on bark paper and sells pottery and the paintings between harvests to the tourists on the other side of the sierra. Beyond that was Mexico City.

Before us the road stretched up across the last mountains before the sea—darkness settled and we could see the first faint lights of other cars moving up along the road that humped into the sky, disappearing on the other side of those dark brown mounds to complete the hundred and twenty kilometers to Acapulco, city of bought luxury and natural passion and removed bliss. And unhidden brutal misery. We were going to Acapulco. Our men were waiting for us there. When the Boy appeared at the window we still had hopes of arriving that night.

I came into the car again and sat down behind the wheel. The infantile mechanic was working with a very serious expression on his face; the self-styled assistant tried to help him find a screw that had fallen beneath the car: "Over to your left, a little further towards Mazatlan, no, closer to Iguala, over toward Iguala, that's it, just a little closer to Mazatlan. . ." Sitting next to me, you had your hands cupping your face, your jaw was resting in them, your eyes were closed. The girl, Bob's daughter was there too in the back seat. She was silent. She didn't complain. It was hard to remember she was only seven. You thought the car would be all right. Sometimes you closed your eyes and swayed back and forth, gently, thinking about it, trying to make it happen.

While they worked and we worked, the Boy came to the window, on the driver's side, where I sat. The Boy's face was very close to my own. He was terribly thin and small and his dark brown head, the exact Mayan features, the very oval black and white eyes, could have been a living mask in the Museum of Anthropology. At once, he was a descendant.

Only his uneven straight black hair was flecked with a few white hairs. He established the fact that he was twelve. He looked six. He could have been five. He could have no age at all. Or any age. Or every age. His arms were very fragile; they hung almost lifelessly at his thin sides but when he slowly moved them, brought them up slowly in some slow-motion gesture, they contained the limits of everything.

126

I looked at his face. At the level of my own eyes I looked at his eyes. He didn't move them away and they were very close to me. I did not touch him but I could feel my lips on his skin, I could feel my tongue around his very dark eyes, a softness closed the distance between our flesh. I did not turn away from him, I didn't take my eyes from him, even when I turned my head his image remained in me. I'm giving it to you as I keep it for myself. I possess it as sharply and as gently now as I write this.

He said "Estoy de pedido"—I am asking. I did not understand that. I didn't understand, he said it so slowly, so carefully and without emotion, I didn't understand, clearly he was no beggar, he was poor enough to ask for anything, he was destitute enough to find use for anything given, but clearly that wasn't the sense of it. I couldn't have given him money. I had an almost overwhelming desire to touch him, to hold and caress him. His lips were several inches from my own. I began to speak to him; there seemed the necessity to speak clearly, slowly, loud and repeating some of the words. His answers were slow, difficult.

He made me understand he was an epileptic. He had fits. "I had one yesterday," he said; "I had one just a few minutes ago," he said again. He watched my face, my eyes. We talked, slowly. As he readied his answers to my questions his face moved up and around, his eyes traveled out on lengths we only sometimes touch. And then we're grateful. Strangely. When they returned to my face as his lips began to form the first syllables of each reply I felt assaulted by the impact of a certain kind of knowledge. The creature was telling me something and I was trying to listen. I wanted to listen as hard as I could.

When the Boy said, "I am twelve," the daughter in the car

began to laugh. She couldn't believe the Boy was twelve. Her head calculated playmates, friends from school, herself—she was seven and twice the Boy's size. The Boy was thinner and smaller than the daughter, by several hands. When you asked me, how old is he, and I said twelve, he says he's twelve, the daughter said, see, you didn't believe it. *You* didn't believe it, you said. *You* didn't believe it, that's what you *said*.

I want to make it clear that he *hung* to the open window of the car. His hands curled over the rim, he was holding on, my eyes conceived of his body as that: head, face, white-flecked black hair, hands and forearms. I leaned over at one point and looked to his legs, his feet, but I don't now have a sense of the lower part of his body. I don't have a memory of his feet planted in the ground. Stance isn't part of my image of the Boy—a close, hovering, floating, that's how I picture him.

His slow, equal, even, separate words continued. His phrasing was the phrasing of music in a funeral march. In that way, with those weighted phrases he told me he had four brothers. Some were older than he, some were younger. He was in the middle. In the middle of four? Then I knew he had said he was *one* of four. There were actually three apart from him. In the middle of four. The gray-brown earth became part of the sky, part of the earth, the sky came down to the earth and became part of it, there was no noticeable becoming, in fact, it was suddenly all one and the only lights were the awkward mechanic's lamp shining at intervals through the space between the engine and the raised hood, the occasional tiny moving lights which were cars crossing the wide hills above and before us to Acapulco, and the great full round yellow moon directly above us.

At that moment I gave the Boy one orange. I took the orange from a bag of twenty or thirty oranges we had in the car and

I put the orange in his hand and the Boy drew in his breath,
I could hear the effort in that act, and all of a piece without
stopping without stuttering or beginning again he said "Dios
te bendiga"—God bless you. And he was gone. Suddenly he
wasn't there anymore. After the Boy left there were other
adventures not part of this story.

TITLES

You write poems with titles, that is you find the title
and then write the poem.
What goes around in your head before you open your mouth
my head in the belly's new electrical orbit .
caught in the refrigerator like a daydream
a collapsible bed.
You missing your friends on the other side of the border
a lot
,the way that frightens me and fills me with your heat
at the same time.
My poems never have titles until the end
and then I have to look for the title and the poem itself
be sure it's there and lately I can't find any.

But seeing M. dying of cancer when no one else knows
like a bright sure terrible light
I am suddenly faceless in front of that, faceless
in spite of the faces alive
all over my body.

THE ANSWER

I'm so glad you came out alive
with your ideas
it's always a good feeling
and your saying I should check the facts,
of course
one should never write without facts.
One should never write.

Or at least not expect it to mean anything
curing sick bones
they will break again
and again.

Your analysis is complicity, yes,
you heard me I'm saying

you are responsible

yours are the words become jargon,
the sadist police, big hinges
on all the doors,
the game
,political, economic or
how to live without giving

anything.

Over the high screech of your words I hear Guevara say
:I used to be a doctor.

—for Che, for Turcos, for Masetti, for Camilo
Torres, for Vazquez Viana, for Otto-René
Castillo and Heraud, for all the others. . .

Only with your eyes
back of a skull that cries
sucking its history
of Green Berets and dogs and special gas
like "Bundles for Britain" or CARE

Only with your hands
fast in a thousand places, here
in every shadow on my face
hands that say goodbye
daily and quickly
convert the oldest gun, touch
lovers and wives and children
who do not come first
for every child's right to come first

Only with your feet
cold in the mountains, hot
from house to house
,your own is moving, every hour
another country
knowing country for what it is

Only with your blood
conscious as rivers   sudden as
hunger again
a suicide devoid of suicide
receptacle going out in that act
continuous blood that doesn't dry
on walls   in dark fields

131

Let LIFE make a story of this
let TIME put its fixed captions
to these pictures
Let them say "love tryst"
or "romantic fool" or "terrorist"
and never say MAN

Only with your bodies
falling against my face
your certain stance
growing along the line of my back
only with these years and years
stretching around the place you walk
and fall
and rise, phoenix again and again

your father's ashes disappear
beneath the only imprint of your eyes your hands your feet

from THE WOMEN

I
The earth won't   will not   can't say that
one thing you can't say   the earth
as it can, it always can, even
one tooth in her mouth and the pavement
hot on the soles of her feet   Even as leather
even as

what she carries on her back
what she has carried   there and returned with
something else   Even this life, the market

the language she speaks
even being Spanish
and not Nahuatl and not Totonaca

Not even through three bad months   till September
for christians, that is to say, men, our men
there isn't any work but will be
It is a future tense   Even as Puebla
maybe she knows it, maybe someone in her family
has been there   the city   but not Mexico City, no

it is sympathy in her eyes
when we say we live
so far from these hills   So other
how to speak   of Revolution   How
it will be night when you get there she says
it will be

goodbye

II
Past the   Here the skin is cracking
the crackling lines around the eyes
flesh of the upper arms   still small, though,
still tight still in-
                        tense, still
the wrong sign   guessing   the wrong house
past house as symbol   house as

past leaning forward   voice going back
into times before the voice the shoulders
how the words made up for it then   made up
the words holding   what wouldn't stay

in one place
She is moving quickly
in her skin eyes jumping around   running
jargon covers wounds and also covers
nothing, sometimes covers nothing
as if out of habit

moving   She is glad to be
forgiven   It is hard   Alone
She is glad   until the cycle begins

again she is glad

III
She has   On her hands and feet
going somewhere else   She is
just this side of that place
knows it better than here though   her minutes
in going   every night every day everywhere
here

the candle burns in her hands   The cycle
is frantic rationale   gripping division
full hair and moon   the image worried
even in her own eyes   the face with tiny creases
of pain

asking the book
asking the clock
asking for definition   forgetting

the answers

THE HISTORY OF BLUE PLASTIC

—for Robert

Once I was seven.
Once I was nineteen or twenty-four.
Once I was cocky and cool and hot
and then I was lost.
Once I was looking for something
and when I found it over and over again
the crumbling shale turned to blue plastic
I was tired
I was tired.

Working hard, an out for it, that white preacher's call
and beginning again
again adding it up in
no erasure, a few extra pounds, the repeated words
sounding above conversation
going out of my head into houses
where all the windows are open.

Try to close the window, try to
close
the window.

It opens.

That last extra shove
and defying that, to live through, the formula
:nothing really matters, being tired
compressed into capsules, the white light,
the lines
working against the face, the taste,
the black hair on the chin, the pounds
more than a few now,
now it's habit.

135

All right.
Everything's all right.

How does it happen then that the door opens, the same door
opens again
someone arrives, the body begins to move,
again real tears come,
the blue plastic recorded in some family album,
the hands
grabbing the handle of that window,
closing it.

Once I was thirty-one.

4/23/67

BECAUSE I LOVE YOU THIS MUCH I CAN TELL YOU

I was strapped to a table face up legs spread
they inserted wires into my cunt
and turned the current on. Did I scream?
It was worse than that I can neither imagine the screams
nor the pain.
Later there is an endless time sitting on a low stool
my legs together.
You are stroking my head one arm around my shoulder
    my head comes
to your groin and I press my head my cheek
against your familiar pants.
That I can imagine and imagine and feel
my whole body and the mind of my body going off on that
forever.
Escape.

This was a dream dreamt awake in my hands my eyes open.
It really happens to Vietnamese women.
Later in a prison camp they cannot even speak of it.
The article ends "They didn't confess you can't make
    a revolutionary
confess."
What I can confess against your legs my sisters' pain
is.

WAITING WITH YOU

—for Robert

I love you.
That's the first line of this poem, like your last. Period.
And all the fear that comes from that, and the no-fear
    heavy, into my eyes.
I hate all the old poems I hate all the books, want to look away
as you turn the pages.
I love you.
No fucking no work no salt no face to the sun the doctor says
for a while
such a little deprivation beside what our brothers and sisters
but when you go I quickly put the Internationale on the
    record player
to lift my body, remembering
that balcony high in Havana. . .
And now the other revolutionary songs on the record are like
    German boots
sinking across my bed.
I love you.
The baby rolls, pushes against the skin of my belly, your baby,
our baby will come when he will.

137

Like our oldest son coming to see us make love
or the tears of our daughters
your ear to the heartbeat your hand between my legs.
A time to crown this waiting.
A time to look the oldest son in the eyes.
A time to place all this
real as the song, the window, the old poems,
my discovering
                    I believe you.

WHY DON'T I GIVE YOU MY MILK

> *There is nothing more suspect than the formula*
> *"to everyone according to his work" in a world*
> *where work is the blackmail of survival; to say*
> *nothing of the formula "to everyone according*
> *to his needs" in a world where needs are deter-*
> *mined by power.*
>
> —RAOUL VENOIGEM, *"The Totality for Kids"*

Anna when you suck on the nipple of the bottle
that small persistent noise brings the milk
to my breasts
the pain with it, obeys the natural workings
in spite of pills and hot compresses
pumps and decision and tears.
Then why
don't I give you *my* milk?
Why did I try as hard as I could
and still feel death in my breasts, empty-handed, cold?
Why am I also relieved?

Anna, Anna, to hold you close to my body. . .

KLEENEX

I remember we never bought Kleenex
(the consumer name for facial tissues)
We never used them because toilet paper was just as good
I can hear my mother saying it
and tearing off a big wad.
There were no associations, just thrift/a sense
of saving.
It set us apart.
In Sheila Anne Turner's house there were facial tissues
to match each bathroom   dusty pink   pale blue
       sunny yellow
her mother was fat her father always smelled of proper drunk
her mother's lingerie drawer smelled of sachet.
Sheila Anne always had the most expensive underwear
the newest adult deodorant the saddest eyes.
She was the first to fuck
and worry about
getting you know
being
making you know
A Mistake.
Years later her Republican senator father
divorced her sad respectable mother
and Sheila Anne waited and waited and waited
and learned to weave expensive original fabrics
and married
finally
a wiry aryan cold Hungarian refugee
who clicked his heels together and drove his MG over ninety
and never spoke.
Pulling another Kleenex from the box to wipe my fourth baby's
banana-splattered chin
I think of our tissueless house and Sheila Anne's opulence.
She once told me she knew I'd have several husbands

you're the type, she said.
At the time it hurt we were Best Friends that was High School
Midwestern America.
Now the bodies feel very warm and very good and his
    especially and everything is
relevant.

SOMEONE ELSE'S HOUSE

I turn the pages and see that some of them many of them
still write about American civil war heroes.
And not because they see any resemblance.
Talking to her voice not her on the phone.
Very one-tone no change except where it almost moves to
    the edge.
Off that edge there is no control at all.
And why does she need it?
Because she's in someone else's house the phone's in
someone else's house
and the baby will probably die on Monday though
    the operation
might work.
She seems so happy now has rosy cheeks the voice almost
    goes that makes it worse.
I can't say anything to her nothing would enter that voice
going. . .

And spend two hours rocking and hugging and pressing
my own beautiful healthy three-week-old baby
wondering if this kind of joy is permissible
under the circumstances. Permissible?
Is someone else's house ever really someone else's?
Allowing divisions. Taking when necessary.

What time?
What heroes? Were they really?
All night I imagine those tiny valves
reversed in her very small heart
which is somehow very different from the night before
when the calm dream voice of your dream father called
    long distance
to calmly say your dream mother's dead and the dream
absolutely flat. Like a fist pried open. Then nailed down.
This one is the tips of fingers.
Long tangled marionette strings all the way up to State.
Control.

How we can't even imagine *they* are immune from that. Here.
Moving the tiny right-hand valve to the left
and the left to the right.
And then waiting.
When I explained it to my eight-year-old son
even my six-year-old daughter knew about the dirty blood.
Running away. Coming back.
I want your mouth and hands filled with last night
when we pressed ourselves into each other
in the middle of the night. Sleep and baby bottles. I want
that to possess you now as it. . .*

* Note: 1. The poem was interrupted by your tongue between my lips.
        2. You said you were asleep and though you remember the
        embrace thought you were hugging a guy from your office.

THE WINSTONS AREN'T TRYING TO SAVE THE WORLD: JUST A LITTLE PIECE OF IT*

I

An ad in a "radical" American magazine. They are pictured in an informal pose. By a grandfather clock. By an Early American staircase. White. Their simple, suburban setting. The Mother, the Father, the Two Daughters. Casual. At Home. *The Winstons aren't trying to save the world. Just a little piece of it.*

There are Apaches on the reservation in Clear Fork, Arizona, who can remember the last, hopeless Apache uprising in 1900. But for Della Alakay, a seven-year-old Apache, the enemy is not the U.S. Cavalry. No, the enemy isn't the U.S. Cavalry. The Enemy isn't the U.S. It's important to remember that. From the beginning. Don't become confused. Don't recognize the Enemy.

She and her people are fighting another kind of war. Nothing to do with the one we all know about. *This time the enemies are poverty, disease and despair.* We mustn't confuse poverty, disease and despair with the U.S. Remember, it's Another Kind of War. *And for the first time in generations, there's a chance that the Apaches might win: thanks to the courageous efforts of her own people and other Americans like the Winstons.* Get that about "other Americans. . . ." Is she her own people? Are the Winstons Her Own People? Are other Americans Her Own People? Is she Her Own People?

---

* Title of a full-page ad in *Ramparts* magazine, November 17, 1968. Everything in italics represents the completed text, in order, of the ad copy.

II

*Anne and Stan Winston and their two daughters live in a
New York suburb 2,000 miles from the reservation. But it's
another world.* A hierarchy of worlds. Within worlds. Con-
trolling worlds. *The Winstons live in a big, old house and
complain about a big, new mortgage. Their girls have a closet-
ful of clothes and "nothing to wear." They have bikes, skates,
games, books, records and "nothing to do."* Like their parents.
Their parents have nothing to do. To do something they
would have to go outside their structure. Outside their
American Way. Open their eyes. Destroy their crooked dream.
Too hard. Impossible. Dangerous. Instead, they aren't trying
to save the world—within their power, if they were interested
—just a little piece of it.

*Della and her seven brothers and sisters have none of these
problems. Her father spends as much time looking for work
as he does working. Sanitary facilities are almost non-existent.
Electricity has yet to reach them. Water is hauled by hand.
Even the barest necessities are hard to come by.* While they
are saving a little piece, the Winstons and all their friends
are making sure this scene remains alive to their direct action.
Everywhere.

III

*Through Save the Children Federation, the Winstons are
helping Della. The cost is $15.00 a month. It's not a lot of
money, but certainly the Winstons could have thought of a
lot of other things to do with it.* A third car? Or just let dribble
away with the rest of their daily expenditures, most of which
are amply designed to maintain Della—and Ho and Demetrio
and Juan—in a charity-receiving position. Instead, they decided to weight the other side of the mind-soothing balance,
just a little. *Fortunately, they thought only of Della first.*

143

To her, these funds make a remarkable difference. She no longer need feel embarrassed about not having shoes, a decent school dress, school supplies or pocket money. Some of the pressure, too, is off her parents, who can now begin thinking about making their home a little more livable. Also, and perhaps most important, part of the money is put into a fund from which the village can borrow to start self-help projects, including better housing and a water system. Wow. God helps he who. . . And all within the American Way, self-help democracy, $15.00 goes a long way!

Already there is a new feeling of hope among the villagers and confidence in their ability to help themselves. Even little Della has volunteered to give some time each week to keep her school playground clean. Not only the best $15.00 worth you've ever encountered, but a liberal indoctrination in the process. Della wouldn't want to become completely self-sufficient under one of those frightening communist regimes. Better to stay dependent. Get the self-confidence that comes from being protected.

That really is what Save the Children is all about. Although contributions are deductible as a charity, the aim is not merely to buy one child a few hot meals or a warm coat. Instead, your contribution is used to give people a little boost to start helping themselves.

IV

Sponsors are desperately needed for other American Indian children as well as children in Appalachia, Korea, Vietnam, Latin America, Africa and Greece. Check that list out! A good way to keep tabs on where we're doing it to them. And learn a little geography, too. And the plunder is thoughtfully followed in every case by a helping hand, a helpful $15.00-a-month conscience-clearing plan.

As a sponsor you will receive a photo and history of the child, progress reports and a chance to correspond. Relax. You won't have to know or touch or feel any more of the truth than that.

The Winstons know they can't save the world for $15.00 a month. Only a small corner of it. But maybe that is the way to save the world. If there were enough people who care. How about you?

How about you?

THE REAL AMERICAN FLAG UNFURLS
WITH THE HELP OF A WIRE FRAME

Moon landing, July 22, 1969 . . .

I THOUGHT OF THE THINGS I'D NEVER SEE THE THINGS I'D NEVER HAVE AGAIN THE MUSTANG SPORTS CAR AND THAT SWISS CHALET IN SOUTHERN CALIFORNIA. . .

A crown on his head. A pain or a thorn in his side. Her side. A baby on her back. His body. A place out west. Out West. A train on its tracks. That's getting away from it. Getting back to *her*. The side of her head. Her hand on his shoulder. No, *hers. Hers.* The song in her heart. No, that's the way *he said it* about her. Not the song in her heart or the cloud with the silver lining or her eyes brimming with tears waiting for his ship to come in (home) or her hand in his. No. None of these. Her baby on her back her garden her gun on her shoulder her her her place in the (no, no, that's *him* again) her on their his well hill stone arm mountain rock walk walk moon moon moon public and private display of grandeur their mistake talk big moon both hands our shoulder straight ahead gun through 98%, or even 100%

BUT WE TURN THE PIG MYTHOLOGY THE PIG METHODOLOGY BACK ON ITSELF IF YOU KILL A FEW PEOPLE YOU GET A LITTLE SATISFACTION BUT IF YOU KILL ALL THE PEOPLE YOU GET COMPLETE SATISFACTION COMPLETE SATISFACTION ALL POWER TO THE PEOPLE BLACK POWER TO BLACK PEOPLE VANGUARD POWER TO THE PANTHERS. . .

Getting back to percentages. What do they mean? In Ethiopia 98% of all the people can't read or write. All the people. And the peasants (read: serfs) must give 75% of their production to the landowner, and the taxes on the other 25%, and the students, the students made a petition and they took it to their president (read: emperor) who is maybe 0.0001% of the people or something like that and he answered by shutting 100% of the schools.

HE SAID AT THE RISK OF SOUNDING RIDICULOUS LET ME SAY THAT TRUE REVOLUTIONARIES ARE GUIDED BY GREAT SENTIMENTS OF LOVE. . .

our hand our love our shoulder our baby our children our garden our grandeur our moon our love our hate our (problems: for instance, the handedness of nature or the things in nature, the handedness of space or the things in space, the left hand of Kant the right hand of the guy who wrote that book. . .weak interactions. . .decomposition. . .the important fall of parity. . .

EARTH TO THE MOON EARTH TO LUNAR MODULE EARTH TO COLUMBIA ALDRIN AND ARMSTRONG YOUR FEET ARE GETTING IN THE WAY TO THE MOON TO THE MOON TO THE. . . CALLING ALL. . .

146

ARE YOU. . .TO THE MOON. . .THE MOON. . .WE
ARE. . .ALL POWER. . . . .POWER. . . . .
PEOPLE. . . . .

Companies like Dupont and Monsanto have been developing
infrared systems of guerrilla detection so sophisticated that
from a plane at. . .altitude. . .even a lite cigarette. . .

A crown on his head pain or thorn her baby back his body
a place getting back to heart about her the song or the cloud
her eyes come in her hand her gun rock walk moon big or
even 100%.

8/12/69

THE DREAM / 1

I keep saying there was nothing afterward, no trace,
nothing to follow, the decapitated man
was not in the papers, was not there
anymore.
You kept going back to the beginnings, the film,
the building that crashed
just missing the car
                        as we drove
the Blowup tightening
in our heads.

The fact is
at twelve-thirty Wednesday night
or Thursday morning
there was a bright red light
a patrol car blocking the inside lane
two policemen standing almost alone

147

in the dark and the sparse traffic
turning out around and then closing in
and continuing. . .

A body without a head
in pale yellow and very dark blue.
There was gut or esophagus or whatever
spews from a severed neck and there was
no head.
And there was the pressure, the imposed pain
of that man on our eyes, in our eyes,
as the past tense registered. Our heads
becoming the act, the thing.

> The morning paper
> too soon
> the afternoon paper
> ,going through the pages
> and the next day
> and the next.

> And you kept saying
> did you tell her
> did you tell him
> about the man we saw
> and I kept looking.

Now I have dreamed about the yellow and the blue
the pale yellow it was almost white

now I have asked if these bodies are the same
as those others
            chemically, structurally,

now I have asked and dreamed.

Now I will know what colors mean.

TWO WHO DON'T KNOW THEY ARE JOINED IN THIS POEM

—for F., and for R.K.

I wanted to go into the sun
where it was warm and could be warm
inside too, your face is the same and it's not.
You told me
to the music of the gaunt men playing ball
and the women walking slowly and the monkey hanging from
    the old tree
you told me

you were born with crooked legs sleeping in braces
and always straight, that later
you couldn't sleep any other way, the blood
of your first sex
the pain
and no climax and no climax—how do you call it? you said—
never reaching orgasm.

I thought of the blame of your parents
which is the blame of society
which is the blame of us all, of me,
and I thought of the no-blame.
I remembered the letter
from a friend who said (as it reached me
this morning)
"You know I feel no fault in you. . . & no fault
in myself, *No Blame* as the I Ching says"
and you said

I still cry when I think of the shock
it was terrible, the pain, the same pain
that makes us love one another
even before we knew each other here.

Who
was to blame for those shock treatments
I thought on the warm grass.

Your pain points in new directions
like your wrist watch you hung on that woman's shoulder
coming out of the public john, and the blame
to be held in our hands
one by one.

11/21/68

ANOTHER STUDY WITH NO NAME*

The boy who looked maybe eight or nine though it was two
fields down and away and maybe you couldn't really tell from
here ran around and around. He ran around a circle of his
own making and then around a tree which joined the first
circle to make a figure eight. A girl who was smaller, shorter
and more delicate in a pale yellow dress, chased him. She
ran behind him and sometimes, because of the size and veloc-
ity of his circles—still assuming they were *his* circles—she
ran in front of him. He was wearing a light blue shirt and
his pants were darker blue. Every once in a while, like a
bird dipping suddenly in its flight, the boy leaned towards the
ground. He touched it or maybe he really picked something
up before he straightened and kept running.

If you want to do it so bad why don't you go do it yourself?
Go get the damned car and do it yourself. So she left the
room. They both knew she couldn't get the car and do it

---

* The repression hits. This was written in hiding. We had just sent
our four children out of the country, for their safety, our mobility. . .

herself. Not that she couldn't but that she shouldn't. His added *I will say I wouldn't advise it though* was superfluous. Again, it wasn't that she couldn't get the car, but that she shouldn't. They agreed she should be invisible. Sometimes the best way to be invisible was by being with lots of people; sometimes it was by being alone. "Hiding" suddenly seemed to bear tangible strings to that childhood game. Hide & Seek. Just as impotent but lonelier. Behind sunglasses or on a park bench. Waiting. Slouched down in the car. Standing up. The hiders and the seekers. And you didn't know what rules the seekers followed.

On the roof she tried to think Had she ever had a pleasant dream, an exciting dream, a happy dream? He had commented on it. Somehow there was a subtle putdown in the assertion. The assertion that she had never had a happy dream, she never had happy dreams. That always-need to be healthy, open, translucent even. Come clear. Were the dreams always heavy or only now? But now, she guessed she didn't. Have happy dreams. They were always vaguely or violently unpleasant, unhappy, frightening. Especially now. Last night there was a skating rink. For a long time she sat bent over her feet, tying the laces of one skating boot, then another. She took a long time pulling the laces on each foot evenly and tight. Then she went out on the oval rink. She was an excellent skater. After two or three moments of perplexity— she hadn't skated in years—she suddenly knew how again. She flew and dipped and whirled. Everyone stood back and looked and applauded. Even Rita. And Rita was the only one who knew she was going to die soon.

The rink became a swimming pool out of doors. Outside. Sun. Bordered by pretty little cabins. The nearest down front on the right belonged to her. The children followed, running. Gregory. Sarah. Ximena. And Anna. Someone carried Anna, a young blonde girl in a Jantzen swim suit. Inside the cabin everything was simple and warm. Everything was for the children. Uncomplicated. The sense of private property had vanished. Her arms were around the children; she couldn't get enough of hugging them, loving them. *See,* she said, *this is where we'll live. The pots hanging on the walls will be to cook our food. There are beds to sleep in and blankets. We'll have everything we need.* Among the pots there were toys. Simple toys, one for each child. Hanging as useful objects among the pots. Gregory's body gradually lost its stiffness and came into hers. Sarah's eyes were focused very intently; the right side of her brain moving her left hand fast. She saw that Ximena's ear had a little pus coming out, again. Anna smiled. She put her arms around all the children. It felt so good.

Where the two children in the first paragraph were running around in the figure eight, now there is no one. The tree is still there of course, inanimate. The very small figure of another child, boy or girl, very small, red on top and black or dark blue on the bottom, can be seen behind the tree. Actually there are several trees and no one takes prominence now that the game is absent. It is a gray day and all the colors are dulled; the palette would change completely in the sun. I have my back to the cemetery where a procession behind a small white coffin repeats itself every day, every day, coming down the hill, every day people talking and not talking and looking away and the tiny white coffin and the people in black with flowers, some of them in black, walking, every day. I have my back to that. Even the possibility of that.

Forcing myself to turn, just a few degrees to my right in the chair, turning slightly to the right so the red brick wall of the cemetery comes into view. There are hundreds of cows. Going down the hill.

In front, across the field. More cows.

The children crowded into my head, coming out of the dream, on the other end of a broken telephone wire, downstairs, someone else's between my fingers and the typewriter keys, the pain of a telegram in their hands, their fingers, the pain on your forehead as you lie there feeling it, feeling it too, holding them in your head, the pain in my stomach, the blood that keeps coming once a week, all from what is imagined but not imaginary—the difference from one to the other—not like the cows at all. The children, getting paler, further away, dimmer.

Maybe tomorrow.
Maybe.
Maybe it will work.
Maybe it will happen.
My hands grow tight, holding onto it even before it comes, protecting it so no one will take it away again, holding, holding tight. . .

It's as if I've isolated the little girl in yellow and her big brother in blue from their house, from their life. I didn't mean to do that. This isn't a dream (no excuse). They are very poor. The figure eight could be an endless tracing of their lives. From this distance it's easy to think of the field and the tree and the cows and the house and the children and the game as a painting, which is a game. A changing palette according to sun or rain. Only the surface changes.

I could never hold that tight because all the blood all the burnt flesh all the hunger all the exploitation of all the people can't fit in my fist. Or can. Would break. Not mine. The hand is forced open. . .

The children come back. The dream starts and stops and starts again. I must break that love open and let all the children in.

8/10/69

153

[Instructions: A kind of play where everything can be re-arranged, the order isn't important, more can be added. The time and the place is now. HE is almost a young executive almost an artist anywhere in the underdeveloped "free" world. Beginning to age slightly around the belly and the eyes. In his early forties, long sideburns if that's currently permissible, short hair if that's currently the style. He dresses conscious of the latest colors and fashions for men and there's a sweet scent, some kind of Masculine Perfume. His face is tender and interested and likable and warm and sad. SHE is at least ten years younger than her husband, tall, a big girl with the face of an aristocratic Roman coin and the eyes of a child. Maybe she's a wild beast in bed; maybe she pulls the covers up to her chin. Her mouth makes a round O when she talks and her hands move and she often prefixes an opinion or a story or a demand or a command with the words no no no no. Taking care of her and taking care of him and taking care of their two small children is CONCHA. Concha's position of power is small compensation for an ignominious salary and life behind the kitchen and before the TV. When she laughs she laughs loud and the whole house shakes.]

Look at the sun isn't it beautiful? From here look at those hills the house going all the way up the cows the fields. Look at the colors. This is the life. . .

Do you like it? Tell me you do. It's yours whenever you want. Of course. It's yours. . .

That was a long time ago we lived in the other house the one Martha has now it was nice you have no idea. I loved that house it was cozy and small no fuss I don't know. Why did we ever leave we were happy yes a beautiful house and Concha lived right down the street seems so long ago. No no no no you have no idea it was good. Those were the days. . .

Ten years ago she wore white socks to her knees they came and a starched uniform every morning a fresh one checkered and starched by Concha. Yes. You have no idea. Even then. Was then she was studying to be a teacher and now she's a teacher but studying still you have to keep up and going to group analysis twice a week with the other two. The two friends. You could write a book! Everything together we do everything together. Same analyst same school. And after ten years you could take a step on your own you could be more responsible you could do something by yourself. With the other two. So the three of them started a school this year. On their own. . .

Do you like it? Tell me you do. It's yours whenever you want. Of course. It's yours. . .

A hundred and fifty pieces of sliced cheese. For the summer camp lunch. Two hundred pesos for tomorrow's sandwiches there's a lot of kids and the money'll go back in. To the school. No no no no. She waves her hand. The problem has to be analyzed from every angle. No no no no. Tonight I'll have my hair done and dress like a matador for the wedding. We've been friends for years you have no idea just for her! Gold and purple purple and gold. Concha will know where the hair spray is, and his cuff links. Come on we're going to be late. . .

Well I know how to treat little Edward now just ignore him that's right and it worked! Me, he said, me, the great Edward and you're not paying any attention, well you have no idea. No no no no. When you have eighty children you have to know how. O they have a marvelous time they run and jump it's great to see. His mother can you imagine at quarter to twelve sent his sweater up. That poor old woman trudging up the hill at a quarter to twelve it must have been his aunt or something and he said Me, what did you send me that for, me? At a quarter to twelve! Afterwards we discuss it the

155

three of us if we have time but so much to do you know how it is every little detail it'll come out in the next group session anyway it'll come out. . .

The little boy who didn't talk till he was three had a wide chest and open eyes. His sister talked backwards earlier. No no no no. With your own it's so much harder. Every day they heard on their mother's knee, here here here, that's it, tight in the arms while the washing machine, there there, but it breaks down. It's all right. How it cost me to learn! What it cost! What pain! So painful you have no idea but the analyst helped me to see, if it hadn't been for him, and then he died. I never forgave him. I almost killed the little one because of it you have no idea she had diarrhea for eight months but I realized it in time. Realized and analyzed. She's a very good teacher and a very good teacher and a very very good teacher. Of other people's children. Learning to cope with her own. A boy and a girl. . .

Do you like it? Tell me you do. It's yours whenever you want. Of course. It's yours. . .

So the analyst's wife took over. Only two days dead and that first session she said O.K., let's see, come on now, closer, that's it, who killed the old man, did I kill him did I kill him is that what you think, come on now! Can you imagine? Wonderful woman. The two friends in the group. I couldn't. But they're not married don't even have a relationship with anyone that's all they have to do. It's different. I have to try to keep the relationship up. He and the children and Concha even. I pay her four hundred pesos that's thirty-five dollars, yes a month, I know it's not much but. From the beginning she starched my. . .

She's hugging me tight and you tight and hugs them tight.

There there. Everything's going to be all right I just know I was thinking about it all the way up in the car well they just can't do that to you they can't it's not right it isn't, Concha! Concha I'm still hungry is that all you're going to give me for lunch, Concha isn't there anything else to eat?. . .

Do you like it? Tell me you do. It's yours whenever you want. Of course. It's yours. . .

He left the house in the morning and went to work. He would have taken the other car but it was still in the shop six months now. Down the hill. A beautiful view from here. The city gets dirtier every day. His office has a painting behind the desk from where you're sitting you can see he uses the telephone a lot. He isn't anyone. He isn't someone either. Not yet or ever. Like research or history a kind of clean law. Not dirty. Advises. Knows. A slightly revolutionary surface within the general context what can you expect lucky to have it. Should be saving money the next regime who knows? And there are meetings and peasants who benefit. Talking about the syndicates made a certain kind of conversation. And you could use it for other things too. The people you met. . .

Sometimes the words form a ball in your mouth bigger and bigger and bigger spills out and you add collect on your chin on your chest it gets bigger and bigger adds to itself and your hands a wonderful storyteller. Do you like it? Tell me you do. It's yours whenever you want. Of course. It's yours. . .

You could talk and talk and there was a knowledge. It wasn't too bad and it wasn't too good. Except out of town with the boss it was all over at three or four. For a late lunch sometimes at home. In the afternoons the rest was yours. From the glass of the studio you can see the cows and the fields and the turkeys and the hills. Somehow the desk wasn't built for holding a typewriter. The only way you can work. But you

157

talk beautifully, you captivate and the others around you when you're not too tired or sad so no use pressing the loneliness. A couple of poems a few years ago in BELLE ARTES. And this collector's item especially bound I wrote the prologue we sold it for the prisoners a kind of political work. I've been working on a series of short prose pieces two years now about animals. In which my father is a beetle. . .

I want to build up a library. I've planned this space where the books will be the shelves are mahogany and this sliding door that's so the dust won't get in more volumes more volume. . .

No no no no. I'm the most bourgeois person I know. And I figure, if I save and save then he goes and spends it on dinner with friends or a drink with the boys, why? Why? I've decided. Everything we need here first, and what's left over, O.K. But there's never anything left over. We owe everything, everything, everyone, a thousand here and a thousand there. He makes eight thousand a month and I make more than one. Mine pays for my analysis and the boy's school. Then there's the short-term loan that's two thousand and the payment on the house and food and we're always a thousand in debt like I said. And Concha, four hundred, of course she's worth it I didn't mean that. . .

Do you like it? Tell me you do. It's yours whenever you want. Of course. It's yours. . .

Didn't you know Miguel? Manuel? Carlin? Armand? He was the leader, yes, these were the years, when that was the big strike, 1958, yes, yes, well I'll tell you. I remember the conversation we had. Five hours. He was the closest to a genius I ever knew. A genius. He's out of the country now got out in time. Too bad. Of course. Even then antirevisionist. And I asked him why we were never on the mark, why weren't we ever there, why were we always late, slow, wrong? The thing

158

is we need the correct analysis. Analyze and then act, that's the problem. To understand the revolutionary situation. . .

I saw her the other day. We had coffee together. She lives by the lake. Yeah, she's O.K. Those were the days. The two of them flew at each other like only women can, positively, they tore each other to pieces. I sat quietly in the corner. It was only my house. Trembling. Like two madwomen they were. Necklaces, clothing flying. Now she lives in the country. Yes. She must be close to fifty. . .

My little girl. There there. My baby. . .

Do you like? Tell me you do. It's yours whenever you want. Of course. It's yours. . .

Come on papa she says. He stands in front of the Victorian cabinet. The one from her mother's cellar. Long ago. Re-arranging the pieces of *art nouveau* one by one. The mermaid in the ashtray was just a piece I picked up for ten pesos then I saw it in the book. Signed and everything. Had it re-bronzed the other day. See here's the signature. He passes it around. No no no no. Just marvelous. And to think he got it for ten pesos. In a market. That's a real prize that piece. For hours he moves them upstairs and downstairs in his hands he moves them in his head with his fingers on them the objects he arranges the new objects old *nouveau*. *Art nouveau* to touch and move for hours to arrange. Holding his loneliness and his emptiness in his hands for people to admire and discuss. . .

In the upstairs hall of the house they've always wanted they bump into each other and their shoulders touch. O. They turn around. Saving for ten years. Still paying it off. They touch and it's already beginning to fall apart and it's only a year. The water coming in when it rains all the time. They touch.

By mistake. The parquet floors buckling, moisture on the walls, the dampness. They touch of course you're never home so you wouldn't know. You leave before I do and come home later. These things need watching they need a kind of vigilance you wouldn't know anything about because you're never here. By accident. They touch. Nothing. No no no no. She smiles. . .

You going to blame the washing machine on me too? Must've been two of them carried it off in the middle of the night. God knows and everyone here everyone right here in the house amazing no one heard. So many thieves around here and the people who live in those caves imagine. No no no no. She said she loved that furniture we have in the livingroom those authentic cane pieces from mama's cellar. Said I could pick out anything I wanted at *Duveliers* and charge it to her account. I thought I'd get that set the one we've always wanted you know. . .

Do you like it? Tell me you do. It's yours whenever you want. Of course. It's yours. . .

He stands in front of the cabinet, loneliness and emptiness in his hands, they admire and discuss, he knows. . .

We're going to see ten hours straight! Ten hours of movies I'm all prepared four aspirin ahead of time come on along it'll do you good!

Ten hours straight can you imagine no no no no you have no idea but I wasn't even tired I liked it that new Italian director is out of sight the way he makes you FEEL and Isadora Duncan we saw her all this week we saw her complete remember the film was bad last time and we couldn't. What the French can do. But Che. No no no no you can't imagine. I couldn't look. What they did to him. And to Fidel. It was just too much you would have walked out like a drunk who

took pills all the time it was out of sight you have no idea
you just couldn't. We stopped the projector we made them
stop we couldn't stand it we just couldn't look. No no no no. . .

Will you keep me company? Will you keep me company
while I fix something to eat? Just a minute. . .

Going to the hospital to see her in the hospital poor thing. . .

Will you keep me company. . .

Come on papa ten hours straight. . .

Do you like it? Tell me you do. . .

Standing *art nouveau* in his hands, people admire and discuss. . .

Those were the days. . .

Of course. It's the only correct revolutionary attitude. And it
cost him the Party. Those were the days. No no no no. Concha
takes care of everything for thirty-five dollars a month. She'll
find the cuff links and borrow a loaf of bread till tomorrow.
Knows all the neighbors, knows the house. . .

Gotta run. . .

Will you keep me. . .

Ten hours straight. . .

Tell me you like it. . .

Art nouveau, loneliness and emptiness in his. . .

Most bourgeois person I know. . .

161

The only correct attitude. No no no no. A hand in front of her
eyes. Waving in front of her eyes. Walking away the expensive house rain on both sides of the glass. He stands with the
mermaid ashtray in his hands. The children fight over a
piggy bank. No no no no.

A DAY

It came at the end of the day almost at the end it was
    getting dark anyway
and it seemed a very long time had been counted
from beginning to end. On the phone
I thought I had seen or heard her name before.
A strange name that turned out to have been on lots
    of envelopes
sent on. She is a friend
of my second husband and is bringing a doll that talks
for my daughter's birthday today.
Between four-thirty and eight this morning
I fed Anna twice
washed out the day's diapers in the bathtub baked
    a chocolate cake
for the same birthday
took two vitamin pills gave the baby hers gave Ximena her
    ear medicine
made orange juice sat with the kids while they ate breakfast
made lunch made formula.
By midmorning I was confused. Not tired but confused.
Laughing came easily.
I was high. On anything.
I mention that he was my second husband just to acknowledge
    the existence

of a first. Something I almost never do.
Getting around to remembering
without fear his existence.
Just after ten a.m. when I brought your juice up you said
"It's amazing how everyone in this house
has been shouting and screaming for an hour
knowing I'm trying to sleep."
You were asleep.
Although you took the four-thirty feeding when I couldn't
and I love you very much
still I was pissed when you said that. It pushed me back a
    few months or years.
In the car on the way to the ice cream
Ximena said "You sure have a lot of freckles
how come you don't have any on your teeth?"
I miss our son who is away in Puebla. The house is
    without him.
I miss his eyes. The way he doesn't listen when he's doing
    something else.
In the afternoon I finally fell asleep. You pulled the curtains.
Five or six times during the day you have given me your hand
and held mine
and the heat between them is more than sleep. A strong joy.
On the Dialectics of Liberation record Stokely Carmichael said
if the U.S. ghettos had been planned like
    the South African stockades
their unified pattern would be less frightening. He's right.
My brother is here
and reading an 800-page anthropology text.
I enjoy falling easily into the pattern of his sense of humor.
It makes it easy to be close to him without waiting.
At 4:38 I discovered
that Anna is now strong enough
to hold the pacifier in her mouth
and digs it!

163

Maybe tonight we'll go to the movies. Your night off.
    I love you.
Later *Bonnie & Clyde* was one of the two best movies
    I've ever seen
and I didn't fall asleep and the real American Myth/Truth
made me homesick.

4/4/69

BOTH DREAMS

I
The girls were not young women. They were
endless children forever playing ball and skipping,
    cropped hair
on ugly thickened faces. Some pimpled faces.
They pushed each other on swings then ran and
    jumped as a group,
their long black skirts swinging, their long blue
    checkered aprons
swinging over their black stockings and black shoes.
I watched them and watched them and my mouth got dry.
I asked you if you wanted to eat them out you said you
    didn't think so.
You said Fellini I thought Viridiana.
So much unwet woman
dying beneath those heavy skirts
turned me on to hot fingers
rubbing those pubic bones caressing the snatches of those
    early Sisters
of Charity.
The dead black skirts
held up by pairs of thick scrubbed hands

like dark proscenium
while my fingers worked, moved, my body moved
in and out of sleep, the water coming
into my mouth.
In Women's Liberation terms I thought of the condemnation
in the word Snatch.
In any real dreaming every real term I saw the condemnation
    of those lives
running out of the mountain park bouncing volley balls
up and into the green station wagon. In they went.
It said
Fudacion Gabriel Ulloa.

II

In the second dream I was walking
heavy coat and scarf and boots, gloves and muffler through
    cold snowy streets.
Knocking on a door I asked for work.
You can clean these two rooms on either side of the hall
the homosexual mannequin said.
You can come every morning at eight and arrange all the
    miniature faces,
counting them, in boxes.
I'm very grateful for the work I said. I opened the door
and went slowly down the symmetrical walk
pushing a wheelbarrow filled with the unknown machinery
    of cruelty.
I walked slowly, in the cold streets, my head
very high and straight ahead
pushing the great machinery of cruelty
in my wheelbarrow
with my hands.

III

You were so tired you fell asleep as I told you both my dreams
my fingers on your back.
I could hear you snoring
suddenly.
I thought of today's forest, the darkness and shafts of sky
coming down between those very tall trees.
As we walked with the children. Leaving the dance of the
    Sisters of Charity.
Behind.
The side of my body was tight to yours my hand in yours.
Afraid of the mushrooms afraid, even, of seeing them.
And you
with your bad knees.
O I want the bright time in my hands and all around us,
your body strong and my head clear of that disaster
in forests we'll conquer because we'll have to.

SOME TRANSLATIONS

In this section of translations, León Felipe was one of the finest of the old Spanish poets still alive until a few years ago (he died in Mexico, still in exile, in 1968). Otto-René Castillo was born in Quezaltenange, Guatemala in 1936 and was killed there in March of 1967 while fighting with the Revolutionary Armed Forces. The poem by Javier Heraud, written in 1963 in La Paz, Bolivia, was one of the last by the poet before his death. Peruvian, he was killed at the age of 21, while fighting for the liberation of his country. Leonel Rugama, another young Latin American martyr, was assassinated in January, 1970 in Managua, Nicaragua. The house where he and two comrades hid was surrounded by 1,500 national guardsmen and the battle lasted 4 hours. Before they went in to finish him off, Rugama answered the demand that he surrender with: *"Qué se rinde tu madre!"* Roque Dalton is a Salvadorian poet living in Cuba. In 1969 he won the Casa de las Américas poetry contest with the book *Taberna y otros lugares,* from which this poem was taken. Carlos María Gutiérrez is Uruguayan. Well known as a revolutionary journalist, *Diario del Cuartel* came directly out of a prison experience in 1969 and is his first and only book of poems. It won the Casa de las Américas poetry prize, 1970. The last two poems in the section grew from the experience of a trip to Vietnam in February-March, 1970, when six Cubans investigated U.S. war crimes and made a film. Roberto Fernández Retamar, the poet of the group, edits the Casa de las Américas magazine and teaches at the University of Havana. The poems by Dalton, Gutiérrez, and Retamar were translated with Robert Cohen.

167

AUSCHWITZ / *León Felipe*

to all the Jews in the world,
my friends, my brothers. . .

Those infernal poets
Dante, Blake, Rimbaud. . .
let them speak more softly. . .
let them lower their music. . .
Let them be quiet!
Today
anyone on earth
knows more about hell
than these three poets together.
Oh, I know that Dante plays a good violin. . .
The great soloist! . . .
But he shouldn't pretend anymore
with his marvelous terzettos
and his perfect hendecasyllables
to frighten that small Jewish child
there, torn from his parents. . .
and alone.
Alone!
waiting his turn at the ovens of Auschwitz.
Dante. . .you went down into hell
with Virgil, led by the hand
(Virgil, the great "cicerone")
and your Divine Comedy was a happy adventure
:music and tourism.
This is something else. . .something else. . .
How can I explain it to you
if you don't even have the imagination?
You. . .you don't have the imagination—
remember, in your "Inferno"
there isn't even one child. . .
And the one you see over there
is alone.

Alone! Without a guide. . .
waiting for them to open the doors of a hell
that you, poor Florentine,
can't even imagine.
This is something else. . .how can I tell you?
Look! This is a place where you can't even play a violin.
Here the strings
of all the violins in the world
are broken.
Do you understand me, poets of hell?
Virgil, Dante, Blake, Rimbaud. . .
Speak lower!
Play more softly. . .Shhh!. . .
Be quiet!
I'm a good violinist too
and I've played in hell many times. . .
But now, here. . .
I break my violin. . .and I'm still.

from LET'S GO COUNTRY (Part II) / Otto-René Castillo

Let's go country, I'm going with you.

I'm going down to the depths you claim for me.
I'll drink from your bitter cups.
I'll remain blind that you may see.
I'll remain voiceless that you may sing.
I will die that you may live,
for your flaming face to appear
in every flower born of my bones.

That's the way it must be, unquestionably.

Now I'm tired of carrying your tears with me.
Now I want to walk with you, strike lightning.
Go with you on your journey, because I'm a man
of the people, born in October to confront the world.

Ay, country,
the colonels who piss on your walls
:we must pull them out by the roots,
hang them from the tree of bitter dew,
violent with our people's anger.
And so I say, let's walk together. Always
with the agrarian peasants
and the union workers,
with he who has the heart to know you.

Let's go country, I'm going with you. . .

BALLAD OF THE DEPARTING GUERRILLA / *Javier Heraud*

One afternoon he says to the one he loves:
I'm going, the rains have come,
the soil is wet
life comes up in my throat
I can't stand the oppression any longer.
While my brothers die in the mountains
by assassin shells,
I can't remain thoughtful,
indifferent.
Goodbye, I'm going to the mountains
with the guerrillas.
He said goodbye and he left.
And one day he was there
up above, shoulder to shoulder with the guerrillas.

His hand was a fine silver spade
ploughing, sowing, harvesting
the earth,
rays of hope
came from his rifle,
and the next day he was dead
with six feet of earth on his shoulder.
Thoughtful and sad
he still remembers the one he loved
for a long time now, forever.
And she waits for him by the river,
on the bridge where she saw him leave.
And she strokes her belly sadly,
thinking of him, of them all,
with her beautiful proud eyes
she looks towards the bridge, the river, life.
And in her heart she feels the hope, the new joy
that her loved one gathered
on earth.

THE EARTH IS A SATELLITE OF THE MOON / Leonel Rugama

The apollo 2 cost more than the apollo 1
the apollo 1 cost enough.

The apollo 3 cost more than the apollo 2
the apollo 2 cost more than the apollo 1
the apollo 1 cost enough.

The apollo 4 cost more than the apollo 3
the apollo 3 cost more than the apollo 2
the apollo 2 cost more than the apollo 1
the apollo 1 cost enough.

The apollo 8 cost a whole lot but you didn't feel it
because the astronauts were Protestants
they read the Bible from the moon,
bringing glad tidings to all Christians
and Pope Paul VI blessed them when they returned.

The apollo 9 cost more than all the rest together
including the apollo 1 which cost enough.

The great grandparents of the people of Acahualinca
    were less hungry than the grandparents.
The great grandparents died of hunger.

The grandparents of the people of Acahualinca
    were less hungry than the parents.
The grandparents died of hunger.

The parents of the people of Acahualinca
    were less hungry than the people who live there now.
The parents died of hunger.

The people of Acahualinca are less hungry than their children.
The children of the people of Acahualinca
    are born dead from hunger,
and they're hungry at birth, in order to die of hunger.

The people of Acahualinca die of hunger.

Blessed be the poor, for they shall inherit the moon.

ON HEADACHES / *Roque Dalton*

It's beautiful to be a communist
even though it gives you lots of headaches.

And the thing is that the communist's headaches
are supposed to be historical, that is to say

they don't go away with aspirins
but only with the realization of Paradise on earth.
That's how it is.

Under capitalism our heads ache
and they decapitate us.
In the struggle for the Revolution the head is a time-bomb.

In the construction of socialism
we plan headaches
which doesn't make them any less frequent, just the other
     way around.

Communism will be, among other things,
an aspirin the size of the sun.

GARBAGE WAGON / *Carlos María Gutiérrez*

I remember the mules in an impossible year
Ejido al Norte
and those great shouts beginning the day
the mules hitting the new asphalt
to Palermo raising their torment my gasp about to cry
and the whiplash like gunshots
and the stopped streetcars ringing their bells

and the wagon tons of filth and garbage
and the squalid beasts their bloody lips
those green trees awkward shouts the foam of the mules

so
among death rattles kicks and roaring guffaws
the garbage rides the hill to another world
to the crematoriums but I didn't know that word yet
I cried for the mules but more because no one said where
    they went
and the sun on *Ejido al Norte* laughing at everything
and the mules' agonized trembling with fury stubborn pride
and me nothing I could do
dumb child crying on the curb

this morning the sun still laughs
and we're going along *Ejido*
there aren't any mules no one shouts no one cracks a whip
the streetcars died along with so many things
the wagon is blue
plastic and steel
but it'll never ring a bell like that one
when it makes its demands its horn sounds in English
the opposition calls it "the chanchita" though its name
    is Chevy*
inside we're eleven and four police
green leaves just beginning
morning light happy and mysterious
we move through shadows we have no cigarettes
last night we didn't sleep
our only breakfast: the photos the files the fingerprints
full wagon without a child to cry as it heads

up *Ejido al Norte* but I don't know where—
they're taking away the garbage that polluted the landscape

* Paddywagon.

VISIT / *Carlos María Gutiérrez*

This middle-aged woman looks at me
chooses her words hands me a chocolate
the sergeant brought the guard's chair
and she sits in the sun
talks for five minutes
woolen socks the oranges are sweet Coca baked you a cake
but there's still an hour to go

the M-1 makes her sad
she doesn't know that green box on the table
is called walkie-talkie and listens to us
she's from another age from a family without prisoners
in spite of everything she whispers furtively
and the soldier comes closer to spy her message:
why the shirt was so badly ironed

this woman is silent
there's so little to say between two old people
she always used to talk to children there were blackboards
every morning one of them brought her a rose
in her country school the sun didn't stick to a schedule
there were no guards with their M-1's cocked
if she felt like crying
she could always explain the diphthongs with her back to
    the hurt
and the chalk took the place of the useless answers
    the pauses

this woman hides behind her dark glasses
remorse in the time that's left
before the last bus back to Montevideo
there are no blackboards
and even the sun is on loan from the Armed Forces

175

this woman looks for a long-gone child in me
and all she finds is a man dirty and a little sick
who escaped from time and is also silent

this woman looks at her watch the time is up
they've withdrawn the sun they're taking the chair away
who was this stranger his beard grown
limping away between two guards?

this woman my mother standing there dark glasses
with her child corpse rotten in her arms

STATEMENT TO THE INTERAMERICAN PRESS SOCIETY
/ Carlos María Gutiérrez

I smile bearded haven't washed for a week
I'd have to take off my sweater disorganize my undershirt
to scratch there where it itches
but I smile anyway
I even thank the cricket who stops singing and fears me
if I had with what
I'd write my gratitude
my joys in 30-pt. type rimmed in an 8-pt. box

what minister of state can stand against this people
what general can force them to carry out his braying
what president will be pardoned when the noose tightens
    around his neck
if Juan's there

of course that's not his name but it'll do

this Juan with his rifle and seven kids
enlisted for a year to get off misery's list

"we're going to give you the lodging you deserve"
said the colonel pistol on his hip italian belly
and all he could invent for me was this dungeon without a
    cot poor guy
at night in the casino he's the one who feels cold on his
    tenth whisky
who can't sleep when he goes whoring
who dies of hunger at the banquets

"here there'll be none of those papers or magazines
none of that marxist bullshit"
recommended the major who actually reads
who learned all the tricks of the press from
    READER'S DIGEST
and when he's in the shower rubbing his groin
his wife in Pocitos
rejects and nurses the fantasy
of Lucy Johnson on her wedding night a PLAYBOY foldout
    anglosaxon breasts
Panama black girl smelling of pineapple*
Fort Bragg in his memory not this dump called Minas

"no newspapers allowed here"
said the ensign blushing and it's only natural
I initiated the boy I'm his first prisoner
sometimes as a student he read my articles secretly
now he sees the gray in my beard my face with runny eyes
he can listen to my old snores smell my solitary nightmares
I'm his first civilian in humiliated state
the only vietcong within his modest reach

    * In English in the original. Imperialism having its effect on the
Spanish language, via United Fruit, etc.

177

"the latrine's in condition"
Juan said in military jargon taking his post
and he looks at his boots avoiding my eyes
immersed in his *mate***
each slow word
pensive *gaucho**** poker face over a royal flush and waiting

then
I've asked permission the request's gone out the permission's
    come back
and next to the john on the rusty nail
is today's paper in careful pieces in hygienic texts

the regulation five minutes
but I read the cables
Armstrong stepped on the moon and says it's very sad
I'll come back later to read the police reports keep tabs
    on the boys
if I make a schedule and nobody else asks to go
though there are a few with hepatitis
I'll get to the obituaries the editorials
before they march us out for the lowering of the country's flag
that old army habit of theirs

I smile grateful to this Juan so poor so soldier
compañero sitting before my door
poet of this beautiful parable about the news and its
    double use

what general minister president
what colonel major young ensign
can stand up against this Juan against this people
against these silent joys

** *Mate* is an herb tea popular in Uruguay and Argentina.
*** *Gaucho* is the cowboy of the *pampas*, the Uruguayan and Argen-
tine plains.

WHAT WERE WE DOING? / *Roberto Fernández Retamar*

What were we doing the 15th of July, 1966?
The date tastes of beach, field, crops, friends.
In the fishing village of Ngu Thuy,
which was a fine place on the Pacific coast,
the 15th of July 1966
the American planes began to bomb,
and they continued to bomb for five days
until all the houses were destroyed
by the sounding Pacific.
What were we doing that day, ignorant ones?

SUNDAY / *Roberto Fernández Retamar*

Among the several ways of spending a Sunday
this Sunday February 21, 1970, we find another:
waiting for them to detonate for us, for our cameras,
a six-hundred pound that will blow up a house.
We begin to wait at nine in the morning.
At eleven we've waited a couple of times, breath held,
      muscles tight.
At twelve-thirty they decide it's better to wait till
      the afternoon.
We have lunch, awkwardly upset.
At two we go out again.
At a quarter to three the cameras are ready once more.
A few minutes later, one shot, another, and another
      (it's the signal)
and the house, five hundred feet away, disappears like a huge
      door slamming,
a red and gold flame surrounded by endless black smoke
rises into the sky this strange Sunday in February.

179

OTHER POEMS / 1970–71

A NEW HOUSE FOR YOUR BIRTHDAY LENIN*

The State must change lodging
from family to family
evict one family to house another
the capitalist State does this every day
and our proletarian or socialist State
will do it too.

The capitalist State evicts a working-class family
that's lost its supporting member.
A policeman appears, a guard or a battalion.
    The eviction notice.
In a workers' neighborhood
to evict a worker
a whole army of Cossacks is needed. . .

In the proletarian State we resort to coercion too
in order to house a miserably poor family in the home
    of the rich.
Our people's militia consists let's say of fifteen people:
two sailors two soldiers two conscious workers
an intellectual eight laborers
and of these, at least, five women. . .
Our army arrives at the home of the rich family,
checks it out and finds five rooms occupied by two men
    and two women.

* Most of this "poem" is a paraphrase of an article by Lenin, published in *Prosveschenie* magazine in October 1917.

Citizens, they say, snuggle up in two rooms while the
    winter passes
so the others can house two families living in the cellar.
Temporarily, until with the help of our engineers
—you're an engineer, isn't that right?—
we can build enough houses to go around
we'll be forced to ask you to double up.
Ten families will use your phone
saving a hundred hours of duplicate shopping, etc.
Furthermore,
the partially usable semiworkers in your family
—a citizen of 55 and a citizen of 14—
will be put to use on daily three-hour shifts,
the just distribution of goods,
your signature,
and the exact carrying out of this order.

The people's State orders the just distribution of goods.
That was Lenin in 1917.
Fidel in 1959 filled the houses with children.
The rich left on their own accord.
And Lenin's lips still move softly, firmly, slowly
drowning out the HOUSE & GARDENS
of the world
                violently
before it's too late.

ROBERT I REMEMBER THAT PAINTING
AS MUCH BY DIEGO AS BY FRIDA

What you look like when you're like that
tight lips squared over your teeth
blood run from your whole face
leaving it pale blue. Pale footsteps in circles
all over your forehead
that spreads out and out of my line of sight.
Eyes with closed hate keeping them open.
You from this open eye of mine.
I am a very small very powerful very stationary sexless being
(though I use myself I'm still talking about you)
standing in the absolute middle of that huge forehead
and you're aiming second-hand bullets at me.
Each bullet contains the whole Revolution
(not as if more or less revolutionary as our errors
      fragment into)
the whole thing in each bullet over and over again.
When you try to pretend that old anger is new
none of the bullets hit
and they pile up around you, the full shells
and finally the explosive pile covers you
(what you look like)
and I can't see you anymore.
When the blood comes back to your face and your
      mouth softens
to speak
you've got perfect aim.
I grow I become a woman (and a man) the way I always am.
We take up our separate instruments again
we didn't put them down
in another poem they'll be weapons.

CLARITA / December 25, 1969

The worst is your face falling away, losing,
I can't see it anymore
can't remember exactly the way it was
as it was,
not puffed up fattened in the coffin I couldn't look
wanting to remember you the other way
but now that's going too
nothing will bring it back
nothing will bring you
not your mother's feet pushing and stamping against the floor
her loud sobs after so much quiet waiting
not your friends' angry eyes
not my son saying Boy were we ever *lucky* we saw her *last*

nothing

FROM THE FIGHTERS / Colombia*

first guerrilla

I'm trying to remember sometimes my memory's not so good
we left Riochiquito when the soldiers invaded the zone
first battle with the *chulos*** in the place called Palomar
    we had one wounded
they had several dead.
And into the high part of the mountain.
That day it rained a lot it looked like the sky was broken

  * Based on accounts by Colombian guerrillas during the three periods
of violence, 1948 to the present. . .
  ** Government soldiers, literally means "pimp."

183

we arrived wet Marulanda our commander prepared
    an ambush
that day on the retreat
the guards abandoned the post too soon and they jumped us.
They wounded Lucio Mesa they took his pack and his gun
but we carried him on. He died that night.
The next day we came to a new canyon between Montalvo
    and Chiquila
Leonardo stayed behind exhausted he lost the rhythm of
    the march
while we waited up ahead
the *chulos* got him and killed him with a machete.
Cruz was numb with hunger he got yellow he never spoke
    again he died.
We came to a farmhouse an old couple man and wife
Marulanda explained why we fought for the Revolution
they sold us some sugar cane.
Marulanda was like a clock
Boys it's time for breakfast each took out his little piece
    of cane
O.K. it's time for lunch again we sucked our piece of cane
Don't forget it's dinner time and the cane sucking continued.
The *chulos* were everywhere.
That night we got out.
The moon came up at last.
The night wasn't so dark.
Nearby we heard noises it was the *chulos* moving in ambush
    we kept quiet
quiet in the corner of the mountain
everyone covered and ready. They came close.
We heard them breathe. . .
Patiently we waited for the night.
At six-thirty we came out we walked till the sun came up
    for a long time
we've been almost without shoes
moving again towards Marquetalia,
breaking the blockade. . .

We were more than 100 colonos this is a very old story more
    than ten years old.
When the army attacked we were beginning to harvest
    the coffee
we couldn't even harvest it.
We divided into three columns one stayed in there fighting
another crossed over to Sumapaz and we began the march
to Guayabero.
The march began in January Guayabero was jungle then
and we told the peasants:
We're from the east we're guerrillas and this is the program
    we bring.
Eight years ripping the mountain apart.
Then the army came in the evacuation began.
I remember the first contact it was the 8th of June.
We were crossing a river by cable when they came and
    told us
another group of families had come from Guayabero. We ran.
There were 62 families some 400 people
18 days through the jungles mountains plains 4 big rivers.
Their clothing was shredded almost no one had shoes.
Seven guerrillas came as leaders or guides the soles of
    their feet
were eaten away.
A child lost an eye an old guerrilla lost his wife and his
    two children
lost along the way they died of hunger and cold.
And now
what can we do?
I want my oldest son to march with the guerrilla leave me
    the youngest
to help me with the work.
After we got the families all up into that region we marched
    our troop

to Guayabero. Up to the high place. It was cold enough.
Coming down a guerrilla discovered the body of one of the
    lost children.
It had rolled off a precipice and was caught in some branches.
Its body was of a piece, its little hands with the
    fingers clenched
against the cold.
It was all curled up trying to get warm, the cold
kept its skin fresh.
We looked at it a long time.
The mother must have left it a moment to go ahead for water.
The child must have tried to walk and rolled over the cliff,
seven years old more or less,
the mother must have lost her way and couldn't find her
    child again.
We buried the child.
And continued.
Eight years ripping the mountains apart only to begin again?
Now Guayabero isn't the same Guayabero. Now it's
    only the war
to the end.

third guerrilla

We ran. I was looking for the rear guard in order to
    get through
the wire fence.
Going over they hit me with two bullets
in the upper part of my right arm.
The others got over without any trouble.
I dropped my weapon, falling after it.
My arm was swelling.
The *chulos* continued to shoot at me each round raised dirt
    near my head.
They shot and roared one of them cursed trying to get over
    the fence.

I heard machine-gun and M-1 fire. I saw
a look of madness in the eyes of one of the *chulos*
his desire to kill me like wanting to stomp a snake.
He came closer. He shot twice more.
Feeling him almost on top of me gave me strength I grabbed
     my gun
and ran.
My arm was like a piece of garbage tangled in the bush.
Where it was caught I had to take the sling from my gun in
     my teeth
and untangle it.
Later there was another *chule* he emptied his gun he left
     me for dead.
I was dumped again I was left like a handful of something.
When they were on top of me I let them have it the first
     one I hit
went down
the other jumped and splayed out letting me have it
     I got him though
and was off again.
Seeing that I had a weapon and was using it no one
     followed me anymore.
. . .erasing the trail of blood. . .
. . .my arm wasn't part of me anymore. . .
I was cold. I couldn't sleep.
In the morning I woke up. A cloud of flies.
A pregnant comrade attended the wound one day I
     almost fainted.
I didn't know how dangerous it is for a woman in that state
     to cure a wound
and especially to look on it.
Later they told me she had a strong gaze as if she were filled
with electricity.
In the afternoon the worms appeared in the wound.
I slept.
I woke.
The buzzards. The flies. The worms. The next day

a peasant found me drawn by the smell and the buzzards.
The flesh began to recede my fingers fell off every day
one of the comrades collected the bones and buried them
the arm was like a yo-yo only my thumb was left the wound
    oozed blood.
When the doctors came they took me to a city I saw them
    cutting the meat
and the bones
I saw how they cured what was left.
I was left with this stump.
I returned to my comrades again preparing again they agreed
to take me with them.
How the *chules* run
our bullets on their heels
how they run!
I'm in the mountains again.
This is my home.

I AM ATTICA

I want to write about Attica
because I am Attica. . .
that was our battle: September 9th to September 13th,
those were our brothers, our voice
shouting:

WE HAVE THE ANSWER! THE ANSWER IS UNITY!

Fifteen thousand brothers
in the blackest hell hole in New York State,
they wanted

adequate food and water
adequate shelter
religious freedom
medical attention
from doctors who spoke their language
uncensored mail
freedom to communicate
with people on the "outside"

maximum and minimum security amerikkka

they wanted the pigs off their backs
twenty-five hours a day
removal to a nonimperialistic country
for all political prisoners who so desired
amnesty
for fighting to be men.

Maximum security amerikkka
leading their minimum security sisters and brothers
black brown and white
together in one fierce cry of

REVOLUTION. . .REVOLUTION NOW!

Sam Melville, age 35, serving 18 years after pleading guilty
to bombing government and business offices in New York:
shot dead at Attica. In April he had written:

> ". . . i am beginning to know the meaning of revolution.
> it is the desire for ecstasy and i think only desperation can
> produce it. those who are willing to yield every last priv-
> elege, who drive themselves to the limits of desperation
> will make the revolution. the problem with the "power
> of love" is that despite its once hip notions, it's tied to

traditional definitions of brotherhood and pantheism. i
don't speak for that definition as it applied in the past
though i very much suspect it. we must move to a place
beyond all known issues. for us, now, it is a terrifying
plunge. it may be easier if there is a humanity to come
—but that's not our motive. what we want is salvation
from a meaningless annihilation. to not be cremated for
coka cola and plastic flags in waving simulation on the
moon. . ."

I am Attica
I am Cellblock D, time heavy on that bargaining table,
men knowing each other in their eyes
in an order born of the strength of truth.
I am the interracial security lines inside those walls
surrounded by the little pig-faced sleepy racist
levittown amerikkka
home to secret massing troops
gathering to murder
while brothers laid out those simple demands
while "authorities" made statements
while the impotency of unequal forces
raged for one of the last times. . .

Because I will be Attica forever.
But we are learning:
our knives spears baseball bats gasoline bombs
and homemade weapons
against your CS and pepper gas machine guns
        12-gauge shotguns
sniperscopes submachine guns AR-15 Army rifles
and your coward's shield,
your lies against our truth,
your stalling against our stand.

But it won't always be that way:

THE POWER OF THE PEOPLE
IS GREATER THAN THE MAN'S TECHNOLOGY!

Here
here in the belly of monster amerikkka
in the pit of her blackest cesspool gut
where Sam Melville learned that:

> ". . . the irony of the amerikan prison system is that it
> IS rehabilitating. . ."

and L.D. read a statement following the demands, that said:

> "We are men. We are not beasts and we do not intend
> to be beaten or driven as such. . ."

and Brother Herb told the negotiating committee:

> ". . .what you are hearing is but the sound before the
> fury of those who are oppressed; when you are the anvil
> you bend but when you are the hammer you strike."

September 13. 1971. 42 dead: 32 rebels and 10 hostage guards,
all killed by the coward power of The Man:
Outside the gates
a black woman reporter called it "shooting fish in a barrel,"
a medic who served in Vietnam called it a "war zone,"
a lawyer called it My Lai.

A sister going down to pay final tribute to Sam Melville's body
said:

> ". . .they don't let revolutionaries live, but they can't
> keep the inspiration they give us from us. . ."

And another sister wrote:

> "Attica. If the murder of George Jackson represented one more chapter in imperialism's unchanging strategy of dealing with the black liberation struggle—killing the best of their leaders, from Lumumba to Mondlane to Malcolm—then Attica is the other side: pure genocide. I can't begin to express to you the kind of heroic revolutionary society that those incredible brothers built in cellblock D. . . .the brothers would pass a cup of watered-down coffee around so that everyone got a little, pass cigarettes around, gave the hostages the best, had built an internal discipline based on democracy and firm leadership, loved and respected each other and felt like human beings. . .a glimpse for us of just how deep the waters of courage run in the people. Attica."

WHAT IS YOUR NAME? a visitor asked.
I AM ATTICA the prisoner replied.

I am Attica now in my promise
Attica in my will
in my rage in my strength
in the place I'm moving to. . .

I am Attica forever
in Sam and Herb and L.D.
in all those brothers who stopped being Attica
because they will always be Attica
because they have given us Attica:

one more winning battle
in our struggle. . .

11/71

192

New Directions Paperbooks

Eugenio Montale, *Selected Poems*.† NDP193.
Vladimir Nabokov, *Nikolai Gogol*. NDP78.
P. Neruda, *The Captain's Verses*.† NDP345.
  Residence on Earth.† NDP340.
New Directions 17. (Anthology) NDP103.
New Directions 18. (Anthology) NDP163.
New Directions 19. (Anthology) NDP214.
New Directions 20. (Anthology) NDP248.
New Directions 21. (Anthology) NDP277.
New Directions 22. (Anthology) NDP291.
New Directions 23. (Anthology) NDP315.
New Directions 24. (Anthology) NDP332.
New Directions 25. (Anthology) NDP339.
New Directions 26. (Anthology) NDP353.
Charles Olson, *Selected Writings*. NDP231.
George Oppen, *The Materials*. NDP122.
  Of Being Numerous. NDP245.
  This In Which. NDP201.
Wilfred Owen, *Collected Poems*. NDP210.
Nicanor Parra, *Emergency Poems*.† NDP333.
  Poems and Antipoems.† NDP242.
Boris Pasternak, *Safe Conduct*. NDP77.
Kenneth Patchen, *Aflame and Afun of*
  Walking Faces. NDP292.
  Because It Is. NDP83.
  But Even So. NDP265.
  Collected Poems. NDP284.
  Doubleheader. NDP211.
  Hallelujah Anyway. NDP219.
  In Quest of Candlelighters. NDP334.
  The Journal of Albion Moonlight. NDP99.
  Memoirs of a Shy Pornographer. NDP205.
  Selected Poems. NDP160.
  Sleepers Awake. NDP286.
  Wonderings. NDP320.
Octavio Paz, *Configurations*.† NDP303.
  Early Poems.† NDP354.
Plays for a New Theater. (Anth.) NDP216.
Ezra Pound, *ABC of Reading*. NDP89.
  Classic Noh Theatre of Japan. NDP79.
  The Confucian Odes. NDP81.
  Confucius. NDP285.
  Confucius to Cummings. (Anth.) NDP126.
  Guide to Kulchur. NDP257.
  Literary Essays. NDP250.
  Love Poems of Ancient Egypt. Gift Edition.
  NDP178.
  Pound/Joyce. NDP296.
  Selected Cantos. NDP304.
  Selected Letters 1907-1941. NDP317.
  Selected Poems. NDP66.
  The Spirit of Romance. NDP266.
  Translations.† (Enlarged Edition) NDP145.
Omar Pound, *Arabic and Persian Poems*.
  NDP305.
James Purdy, *Children Is All*. NDP327.
Raymond Queneau, *The Bark Tree*. NDP314.
Carl Rakosi, *Amulet*. NDP234.
  Ere-Voice. NDP321.
M. Randall, *Part of the Solution*. NDP350.
John Crowe Ransom, *Beating the Bushes*.
  NDP324.
Raja Rao, *Kanthapura*. NDP224.
Herbert Read, *The Green Child*. NDP208.
P. Reverdy, *Selected Poems*. NDP346.
Kenneth Rexroth, *Assays*. NDP113.
  An Autobiographical Novel. NDP281.
  Bird in the Bush. NDP80.
  Collected Longer Poems. NDP309.
  Collected Shorter Poems. NDP243.
  Love and the Turning Year. NDP308.
  100 Poems from the Chinese. NDP192.
  100 Poems from the Japanese.† NDP147.

Charles Reznikoff, *By the Waters of Manhattan*.
  NDP121.
  Testimony: The United States 1885-1890.
  NDP200.
Arthur Rimbaud, *Illuminations*.† NDP56.
  Season in Hell & Drunken Boat.† NDP97.
Saikaku Ihara, *The Life of an Amorous*
  Woman. NDP270.
St. John of the Cross, *Poems*. NDP341.
Jean-Paul Sartre, *Baudelaire*. NDP233.
  Nausea. NDP82.
  The Wall (Intimacy). NDP272.
Delmore Schwartz, *Selected Poems*. NDP241.
Stevie Smith, *Selected Poems*. NDP159.
Gary Snyder, *The Back Country*. NDP249.
  Earth House Hold. NDP267.
  Regarding Wave. NDP306.
Enid Starkie, *Arthur Rimbaud*. NDP254.
Stendhal, *Lucien Leuwen*.
  Book II: *The Telegraph*. NDP108.
Jules Supervielle, *Selected Writings*.† NDP209.
W. Sutton, *American Free Verse*. NDP351.
Dylan Thomas, *Adventures in the Skin Trade*.
  NDP183.
  A Child's Christmas in Wales. Gift Edition.
  NDP181.
  Collected Poems 1934-1952. NDP316.
  The Doctor and the Devils. NDP297.
  Portrait of the Artist as a Young Dog.
  NDP51.
  Quite Early One Morning. NDP90.
  Under Milk Wood. NDP73.
Lionel Trilling, *E. M. Forster*. NDP189.
Martin Turnell, *Art of French Fiction*. NDP251.
  Baudelaire. NDP336.
Paul Valéry, *Selected Writings*.† NDP184.
Vernon Watkins, *Selected Poems*. NDP221.
Nathanael West, *Miss Lonelyhearts &*
  Day of the Locust. NDP125.
George F. Whicher, tr.,
  The Goliard Poets.† NDP206.
J. Willett, *Theatre of Bertolt Brecht*. NDP244.
J. Williams, *An Ear in Bartram's Tree*. NDP335.
Tennessee Williams, *Hard Candy*. NDP225.
  Camino Real. NDP301.
  Dragon Country. NDP287.
  The Glass Menagerie. NDP218.
  In the Winter of Cities. NDP154.
  One Arm & Other Stories. NDP237.
  The Roman Spring of Mrs. Stone. NDP271.
  Small Craft Warnings. NDP348.
  27 Wagons Full of Cotton. NDP217.
William Carlos Williams,
  The William Carlos Williams Reader.
  NDP282.
  The Autobiography. NDP223.
  The Build-up. NDP259.
  The Farmers' Daughters. NDP106.
  Imaginations. NDP329.
  In the American Grain. NDP53.
  In the Money. NDP240.
  Many Loves. NDP191.
  Paterson. Complete. NDP152.
  Pictures from Brueghel. NDP118.
  The Selected Essays. NDP273.
  Selected Poems. NDP131.
  A Voyage to Pagany. NDP307.
  White Mule. NDP226.
Yvor Winters,
  Edwin Arlington Robinson. NDP326.
John D. Yohannan,
  Joseph and Potiphar's Wife. NDP262.

Complete descriptive catalog available free on request from
New Directions, 333 Sixth Avenue, New York 10014.   † Bilingual.